Learn ECMAScript
Second Edition

Discover the latest ECMAScript features in order to write cleaner code and learn the fundamentals of JavaScript

Mehul Mohan

Narayan Prusty

BIRMINGHAM - MUMBAI

Learn ECMAScript
Second Edition

Commissioning Editor: Amarabha Banerjee
Acquisition Editor: Noyonika Das
Content Development Editor: Gauri Pradhan
Technical Editor: Leena Patil
Copy Editor: Safis Editing
Project Coordinator: Sheejal Shah
Proofreader: Safis Editing
Indexer: Tejal Daruwale Soni
Graphics: Jason Monteiro
Production Coordinator: Arvindkumar Gupta

First published: August 2015
Second edition: February 2018

Production reference: 1230218

Published by Packt Publishing Ltd.
Livery Place
35 Livery Street
Birmingham
B3 2PB, UK.

ISBN 978-1-78862-006-2

www.packtpub.com

mapt.io

Mapt is an online digital library that gives you full access to over 5,000 books and videos, as well as industry leading tools to help you plan your personal development and advance your career. For more information, please visit our website.

Why subscribe?

- Spend less time learning and more time coding with practical eBooks and Videos from over 4,000 industry professionals
- Improve your learning with Skill Plans built especially for you
- Get a free eBook or video every month
- Mapt is fully searchable
- Copy and paste, print, and bookmark content

PacktPub.com

Did you know that Packt offers eBook versions of every book published, with PDF and ePub files available? You can upgrade to the eBook version at www.PacktPub.com and as a print book customer, you are entitled to a discount on the eBook copy. Get in touch with us at service@packtpub.com for more details.

At www.PacktPub.com, you can also read a collection of free technical articles, sign up for a range of free newsletters, and receive exclusive discounts and offers on Packt books and eBooks.

Contributors

About the authors

Mehul Mohan is an independent developer and likes to develop useful things. He has been working with JavaScript for over 5 years in multiple environments, such as mobile apps, frontend, and backend. He likes to learn and use new languages and frameworks. He runs *Codedamn*, his YouTube channel, which was started as a programming hobby but has been growing since then to teach various programming languages to millions of people. He's currently pursuing his bachelor's degree in computer science at BITS, Goa.

> *To my friends and family, your support and encouragement is much more than I can express here. To mom (Mrs. Ritu Mohan) and dad (Mr. Vinay K. Mohan)—thank you for your evergreen support and moral support that you both have given me over the years.Thank you to my sister (Ms. Ishumita Mohan) for being always there with a word of encouragement or advice whenever I needed it.*

Narayan Prusty is a full-stack developer with 5 years of experience. He specializes in Blockchain, Cloud, and JavaScript. His commitment has allowed him to build scaleable products for startups, governments, and enterprise across India, Singapore, USA, and UAE. At present, Ethereum, Bitcoin, Hyperledger Fabric 1.0, IPFS, Ripple, and so on are some of the things he uses on regular basics to build decentralized applications. Currently he is a full time Full-Stack and Blockchain Engineer at ConsenSys Enterprise. He starts working on something immediately if he feels it's exciting and solves real work problem. He build a MP3 search engine at the age of 18 and since then he has build various other applications which are used by people around the globe. His ability to build scaleable applications from top-to-bottom is what makes him special. Currently he is on a mission to make things easier, faster, and cheaper using blockchain technology. And also he is looking at possibilities to prevent corruptions, fraud, and bring transparency to the world using blockchain technology.

About the reviewer

Domenico Luciani, is a 25-year-old young passionate programmer, currently working as a software engineer for XPeppers, performing extreme programming. He graduated in computer science from the university of Palermo. He is a computer vision enthusiast and loves security, and in his free time, he takes part in bounty programs, hackathons, and dedicated open source events.

Packt is searching for authors like you

If you're interested in becoming an author for Packt, please visit `authors.packtpub.com` and apply today. We have worked with thousands of developers and tech professionals, just like you, to help them share their insight with the global tech community. You can make a general application, apply for a specific hot topic that we are recruiting an author for, or submit your own idea.

Table of Contents

Preface

JavaScript is an integral part of web development and server-side programming. Understanding the fundamentals of JavaScript can not only help a person create interactive web applications but also help set up web servers, create mobile applications through frameworks such as React Native, and even create desktop applications using frameworks such as electronJS.

This book introduces the fresh and core concepts of JavaScript in the form of ECMAScript 2017 (ES8), which includes everything you'll need to get started with JavaScript and have a basic-to-advanced understanding so that you can implement everything mentioned in the first paragraph.

Who this book is for

This book is for anybody who is absolutely new to JavaScript and is willing to learn this technology. This book can also be used by people who are familiar with old JavaScript and want to level up their knowledge to the latest standard and use techniques. For more advanced users, this book can be used to brush up concepts such as modularity, web workers, and shared memory.

What this book covers

`Chapter 1`, *Getting Started with ECMAScript*, discusses what ECMAScript really is and why we call it ECMAScript and not JavaScript. It also discusses how to create variables, perform basic operations, and provides new ways to do those operations in ES8.

`Chapter 2`, *Knowing Your Library*, demonstrates all the functions you need to know as a beginner and intermediate JavaScript developer to work smoothly on various kinds of projects. The functions taught in this chapter are universal and generic functions, which you'll be able to understand and apply anywhere they're necessary for your code.

`Chapter 3`, *Using Iterators*, covers how to iterate over iteratable things in JavaScript the proper way. We discuss Symbol, a new native JavaScript type, what it is, and why we need it. We also discuss the tail call optimization technique, which is implemented by browsers to speed up the code.

`Chapter 4`, *Asynchronous Programming*, explores modern ways to implement asynchronous programming and compares it with the not-so-beautiful past approaches, which included callback hell. It'll teach you about implementing asynchronous programming in a synchronous way.

`Chapter 5`, *Modular Programming*, discusses modularizing your JavaScript code into different files so that it is easy to reuse and debug individual modules. We start with primitive and third-party solutions available earlier and then cover the native support browsers are bringing to the world.

`Chapter 6`, *Implementing the Reflect API*, demonstrates information about the Reflect API provided in JavaScript, which basically helps to manipulate the properties and methods of the objects.

`Chapter 7`, *Proxies*, introduces a new implementation in JavaScript, that is, proxies over objects. It has a number of advantages, such as hiding private properties, setting default values for object properties and methods, and making awesome custom features. Such as Python-like array slicing for JavaScript.

`Chapter 8`, *Classes*, explores classes, how they're implemented, inheritance in classes, and how finally classes is just a syntatic sugar over the function implementation only. This is important because classes make the code more readable and understandable to people coming from an OOP background.

`Chapter 9`, *JavaScript on the Web*, explores the basics of using JavaScript on websites, some popular APIs exposed by browser on the web to the developers, and how JavaScript can be used to interact with the DOM to manipulate things on a web page.

`Chapter 10`, *Storage APIs in JavaScript*, explores the available storage APIs in web browsers and shows how to make use of them to store data locally on the user's computer.

`Chapter 11`, *Web and Service Workers*, discusses web workers available in HTML5, service workers for progressive web apps, and shows how to use these workers efficiently to distribute loads of tasks.

`Chapter 12`, *Shared Memory and Atomics*, teaches us how to harness a multithreaded environment provided by web workers using shared memory to allow blazingly fast access to memory by the web workers through `SharedArrayBuffer`. It covers some of the common problems related to threads sharing the same data, and also provides solutions to those problems.

To get the most out of this book

Although it's not strictly required, it'll be great if you know a little about HTML/CSS and a little about how to create basic web pages using it.

You should be familiar with a modern browser (Chrome or Firefox is preferred) on a desktop/laptop.

To get the most out of this book, don't just read the book alone; keep other study sources open and implement as many of the demo and example codes as you can.

Download the example code files

You can download the example code files for this book from your account at `www.packtpub.com`. If you purchased this book elsewhere, you can visit `www.packtpub.com/support` and register to have the files emailed directly to you.

You can download the code files by following these steps:

1. Log in or register at `www.packtpub.com`.
2. Select the **SUPPORT** tab.
3. Click on **Code Downloads & Errata**.
4. Enter the name of the book in the **Search** box and follow the onscreen instructions.

Once the file is downloaded, please make sure that you unzip or extract the folder using the latest version of:

- WinRAR/7-Zip for Windows
- Zipeg/iZip/UnRarX for Mac
- 7-Zip/PeaZip for Linux

The code bundle for the book is also hosted on GitHub at `https://github.com/PacktPublishing/Learn-ECMAScript-Second-Edition`. In case there's an update to the code, it will be updated on the existing GitHub repository.

We also have other code bundles from our rich catalog of books and videos available at `https://github.com/PacktPublishing/`. Check them out!

Conventions used

There are a number of text conventions used throughout this book.

`CodeInText`: Indicates code words in text, database table names, folder names, filenames, file extensions, pathnames, dummy URLs, user input, and Twitter handles. Here is an example: "Look carefully, we are not executing `counter()` again and again."

A block of code is set as follows:

```
let myCounter = counter(); // returns a function (with count = 1)
myCounter(); // now returns 2
myCounter(); // now returns 3
```

When we wish to draw your attention to a particular part of a code block, the relevant lines or items are set in bold:

```
var ob1 = {
   prop1 : 1,
    prop2 : {
        prop2_1 : 2
    }
};
Object.freeze( ob1 );
```

Bold: Indicates a new term, an important word, or words that you see onscreen. For example, words in menus or dialog boxes appear in the text like this. Here is an example: "However, you can specify the distance to move, that is `history.go(5);` is equivalent to the user hitting the **forward** button in the browser five times."

Warnings or important notes appear like this.

Tips and tricks appear like this.

Get in touch

Feedback from our readers is always welcome.

General feedback: Email `feedback@packtpub.com` and mention the book title in the subject of your message. If you have questions about any aspect of this book, please email us at `questions@packtpub.com`.

Errata: Although we have taken every care to ensure the accuracy of our content, mistakes do happen. If you have found a mistake in this book, we would be grateful if you would report this to us. Please visit `www.packtpub.com/submit-errata`, selecting your book, clicking on the Errata Submission Form link, and entering the details.

Piracy: If you come across any illegal copies of our works in any form on the Internet, we would be grateful if you would provide us with the location address or website name. Please contact us at copyright@packtpub.com with a link to the material.

If you are interested in becoming an author: If there is a topic that you have expertise in and you are interested in either writing or contributing to a book, please visit `authors.packtpub.com`.

Reviews

Please leave a review. Once you have read and used this book, why not leave a review on the site that you purchased it from? Potential readers can then see and use your unbiased opinion to make purchase decisions, we at Packt can understand what you think about our products, and our authors can see your feedback on their book. Thank you!

For more information about Packt, please visit `packtpub.com`.

1
Getting Started with ECMAScript

ECMAScript 2017 (**ES8**) was released at the end of June 2017 by **Technical Committee number 39** (**TC39**). It's part of ECMA, the institution that standardizes the JavaScript language under the ECMAScript specification. Currently, the standard aims to publish a new ES specification version once a year. ES6 was published in 2015 and ES7 was published in 2016. A lot changed when ES6 was released (arrow functions, classes, generators, module loaders, async programming, and so on) and even more interesting stuff keeps happening, as time goes by.

In this chapter, we'll be starting off with the fundamentals of JavaScript, starting off with ES6 basics and heading towards ES8 stuff. Furthermore, we'll be taking a look at some interesting aspects of traditional JS such as closures, and some new ones such as arrow functions.

As an autodidact, I highly recommend not only reading this book, but also trying to apply whatever you're learning here in some small but interesting projects. This will help you to retain a lot of stuff effortlessly.

In this chapter, we'll be covering:

- Creating block-scoped variables using the `let` keyword
- Creating constant variables using the `const` keyword
- The spread operator and the rest parameter
- Hoisting
- Extracting data from iterables and objects using a destructuring assignment

- Arrow functions
- Closures and how to deal with them
- Use of semicolons in JavaScript
- Benchmarking `let` versus `var` versus `const`
- The new syntaxes for creating object properties

The let keyword

The `let` keyword is used to declare a block-scoped variable (more on this later), optionally initializing it to a value. Programmers who come from a different programming language background, but are new to JavaScript, often end up writing error-prone JavaScript programs, believing that the JavaScript variables created using the traditional `var` keyword are block-scoped. Almost every popular programming language has the same set of rules when it comes to the variable scopes, but JavaScript acts a bit differently due to a lack of block-scoped variables. Due to the fact that JavaScript variables are not block-scoped, there are chances of memory leaks and JavaScript programs are harder to read and debug.

Declaring function-scoped variables

The JavaScript variables that are declared using the `var` keyword are called **function-scoped variables**. Function-scoped variables are accessible globally to the script, that is, throughout the script, if declared outside a function. Similarly, if the function scoped variables are declared inside a function, then they become accessible throughout the function, but not outside the function. Let's take a look at an example:

```
var a = 12; // accessible everywhere
function myFunction() {
  console.log(a); // alerts 12
  var b = 13;
  if(true) {
    var c = 14; // this is also accessible throughout the function!
    alert(b); // alerts 13
  }
  alert(c); // alerts 14
}
myFunction();
alert(b); // alerts undefined
```

Clearly, variables initialized inside a function are restricted inside that function only. However, variables declared in a block scope (that is, inside curly braces `{ }` that is not a function (that is, `if` statements)) can be used outside those blocks as well.

Declaring block-scoped variables

Variables that are declared using the `let` keyword are called **block-scoped variables**. Block-scoped variables behave the same way as function-scoped variables when declared outside a function, that is, they are accessible globally. But when block-scoped variables are declared inside a block, they are accessible inside the block that they are defined in (and also any sub-blocks) but not outside the block:

```
let a = 12; // accessible everywhere
function myFunction() {
  console.log(a); // alerts 12
  let b = 13;
  if(true) {
    let c = 14; // this is NOT accessible throughout the function!
    alert(b); // alerts 13
  }
  alert(c); // alerts undefined
}
myFunction();
alert(b); // alerts undefined
```

Study the code carefully. This is the same as the preceding example, but with `var` replaced by `let` everywhere. Observe how C alerts `undefined` now (`let` makes it inaccessible outside `if {}`).

Re-declaring variables

When you declare a variable using the `var` keyword that is already declared using the `var` keyword (in the same scope) then it's **overwritten**. Consider this example:

```
var a = 0;
var a = 1;
alert(a); // alerts 1
function myFunction() {
 var b = 2;
 var b = 3;
 alert(b); // alerts 3
}
```

```
myFunction();
```

The result is as expected. But the variables created using the `let` keyword don't behave in the same way.

When you declare a variable using the `let` keyword that is already declared using the `let` keyword in the same scope, then it throws a **SyntaxError exception**. Consider this example:

```
let a = 0;
let a = 1; // SyntaxError
function myFunction() {
 let b = 2;
 let b = 3; // SyntaxError
 if(true) {
    let c = 4;
    let c = 5; // SyntaxError
 }
}
myFunction();
```

When you declare a variable with a name that's already accessible in a function (or inner function), or is a sub-block using `var` or the `let` keyword respectively, then it's a different variable. Here, is an example this shows the behavior:

```
var a = 1;
let b = 2;
function myFunction() {
  var a = 3; // different variable
  let b = 4; // different variable
  if(true) {
    var a = 5; // overwritten
    let b = 6; // different variable
    console.log(a); // 5
    console.log(b); // 6
}
    console.log(a); // 5
    console.log(b); // 4
}
myFunction();
console.log(a);
console.log(b);
```

Closures and let keyword

Congratulations on making it to here! Let's face it, JavaScript has got some weird (and some bad) sides. **Closures** are on the weird side of JavaScript. Let's see what the term closure actually means.

When you declare a local variable, that variable has a restricted scope, that is, it cannot be used outside that particular scope within which it is declared (depends on `var` and `let`). As discussed earlier, local variables are not available outside the block (as in the case of `let`) or function scope (as in the case of `var` or `let`).

Let's take a look at the following example to understand what the preceding paragraph states:

```
function() {
  var a = 1;
  console.log(a); // 1
}
console.log(a); // Error
```

When a function is fully executed, that is, has returned its value, its local variables are no longer required and cleaned from memory. However, a closure is a *persistent local variable scope*.

Consider the following example:

```
function counter () {
  var count = 0;
  return function () {
    count += 1;
    return count;
  }
}
```

Clearly, the returned function makes use of the local variable to the `counter()` function. What happens when you call counter?

```
let myCounter = counter(); // returns a function (with count = 1)
myCounter(); // now returns 2
myCounter(); // now returns 3
```

Look carefully, we are not executing `counter()` again and again. We stored the returned value of the `counter` in the `myCounter` variable and then kept calling the returned function.

The returned `myCounter` function will count up by one each time it's called. When you call `myCounter()`, you are executing a function that contains a reference to a variable (`count`), which exists in a parent function and technically should've been destroyed after its complete execution. However, JavaScript preserves used variables inside a returned function in a kind of different stack. This property is called a closure.

Closures have been around for a long time, so what's different? Using it with the `let` keyword. Have a look at this one:

```
for(var i=0;i<5;i++){
  setTimeout(function() {
    console.log(i);
  }, 1000);
}
```

The output will be:

```
5 5 5 5 5
```

Why? Because till the time `setTimeout` fires, the loop has already ended and the `i` variable was already `5`. But this does not happen with `let`:

```
for(let i=0;i<5;i++){
  setTimeout(function() {
    console.log(i);
  }, 1000);
}
```

Output:

```
0 1 2 3 4
```

The fact that `let` binds variables to the block (thus, in this case, the `for` loop) means that it binds the variable to every iteration. So, when the loop is finished, you have five `setTimeout` functions (with `i` = `0`, `1`, `2`, `3`, `4`) waiting to fire one after another.

`let` achieves this by creating a closure of its own in every iteration. This happens behind the scenes with `let`, so you do not need to code that aspect.

To fix this code without `let`, we'll need to create an **Immediately Invoked Function Expression** (**IIFE**), which looks something like this:

```
for(var i=0;i<5;i++){
  (function(arg) {
    setTimeout(function() {
      console.log(arg);
```

```
    }, 1000);
  }(i));
}
```

This is more or less what `let` does behind the scenes. So what happened here?

We created an anonymous function that is immediately invoked at every loop cycle with the correct `i` value associated with it. Now, this function has the correct `i` value passed as `arg` in the function argument. Finally, we use `console.log` after a second to get the correct output as `0 1 2 3 4`.

So you can observe, a simple `let` statement can simplify the code a lot in such cases.

The const keyword

Using the `const` keyword, you can create variables that cannot change their values (hence they're called **constants**) once they're initialized, that is, you cannot reinitialize them with another value later in your code.

If you try to reinitialize a `const` variable, a read-only exception is thrown. Furthermore, you cannot just declare and not initialize a `const` variable. It'll also throw an exception.

For instance, you might want your JavaScript to crash if someone tries to change a particular constant, say `pi`, in your calculator. Here's how to achieve that:

```
const pi = 3.141;
pi = 4; // not possible in this universe, or in other terms,
        // throws Read-only error
```

The scope of const variables

The `const` variables are block-scoped variables, that is, they follow the same scoping rules as the variables that are declared using the `let` keyword. The following example demonstrates the scope of the constant variables:

```
const a = 12; // accessible globally
function myFunction() {
  console.log(a);
  const b = 13; // accessible throughout function
  if(true) {
    const c = 14; // accessible throughout the "if" statement
    console.log(b);
```

```
    }
  console.log(c);
  }
  myFunction();
```

The output of the preceding code is:

```
12
13
ReferenceError Exception
```

Here, we can see that constant variables behave in the same way as block-scoped variables when it comes to scoping rules.

Referencing objects using constant variables

When we assign an object to a variable, the reference of the object is what the variable holds and not the object itself. So, when assigning an object to a constant variable, the reference of the object becomes constant to that variable and not to the object itself. Therefore, the object is mutable.

Consider this example:

```
const a = {
  name: "Mehul"
};
console.log(a.name);
a.name = "Mohan";
console.log(a.name);
a = {}; //throws read-only exception
```

The output of the preceding code is:

```
Mehul
Mohan
<Error thrown>
```

In this example, the `a` variable stores the address (that is, reference) of the object. So the address of the object is the value of the `a` variable, and it cannot be changed. But the object is mutable. So when we tried to assign another object to the `a` variable, we got an exception as we were trying to change the value of the `a` variable.

When to use var/let/const

The difference between `const` and `let` is that `const` makes sure that rebinding will not happen. That means you cannot reinitialize a `const` variable, but a `let` variable can be reinitialized (but not redeclared).

Within a particular scope, a `const` variable always refers to the same object. Because `let` can change its value at runtime, there is no guarantee that a `let` variable always refers to the same value. Therefore, as a rule of thumb, you can (not strictly) follow these:

- Use `const` by default if you know that you'll not change the value (max performance boost)
- Only use `let` if you think reassignment is required/can happen somewhere in your code (modern syntax)
- Avoid using `var` (`let` does not create global variables when defined in a block scope; this makes it less confusing for you if you come from a C, C++, Java, or any similar background)

Let versus var versus const performance benchmarks

Currently, running a benchmark test on my own laptop (MacBook Air, Google Chrome Version 61.0.3163.100 (official build) (64-bit)) produces the following result:

Clearly, performance-wise on Chrome, **let** on the global scope is slowest, while `let` inside a block is fastest, and so is **const**.

First of all, the aforementioned benchmark tests are performed by running a loop 1000 x 30 times and the operation performed in the loop was appending a value to an array. That is, the array starts from [1], then becomes [1,2] in the next iteration, then [1,2,3], and so on.

What do the results mean? One inference we can draw from these results is that `let` is slower in a `for` loop when used inside the declaration: `for(let i=0;i<1000;i++)`.

This is because `let` is redeclared every time for each iteration (relate this to the closure section you read earlier), whereas `for(var i=0;i<1000;i++)` declares the `i` variable for the whole block of code. This makes `let` a bit slower when used in a loop definition.

However, when `let` is not used inside the loop body but declared outside the loop, it performs quite well. For example:

```
let myArr = [];
for(var i = 0;i<1000;i++) {
   myArr.append(i);
}
```

This will give you the best results. However, if you're not performing tens of hundreds of iterations, it should not matter.

Immutability in JavaScript

Immutability, defined in a single line, means that once that value is assigned, then it can never be *changed*:

```
var string1 = "I am an immutable";
var string2 = string1.slice(4, 8);
```

`string1.slice` does not change the value of `string1`. In fact, no string methods change the string they operate on, they all return new strings. The reason is that strings are immutable—they cannot change.

Strings are not the only immutable entity in JavaScript. Numbers, too, are immutable.

Object.freeze versus const

Earlier, we saw that even if you create objects with `const` in front of them, a programmer is still able to modify its properties. This is because `const` creates an immutable binding, that is, you cannot assign a new value to the binding.

Therefore, in order to truly make objects constants (that is, unmodifiable properties), we have to use something called `Object.freeze`. However, `Object.freeze` is, again, a shallow method, that is, you need to recursively apply it on nested objects to protect them. Let's clear this up with a simple example.

Consider this example:

```
var ob1 = {
   prop1 : 1,
    prop2 : {
        prop2_1 : 2
    }
};
Object.freeze( ob1 );

const ob2 = {
   prop1 : 1,
    prop2 : {
        prop2_1 : 2
    }
}

ob1.prop1 = 4; // (frozen) ob1.prop1 is not modified
ob2.prop1 = 4; // (const) ob2.foo gets modified

ob1.prop2.prop2_1 = 4; // (frozen) modified, because ob1.prop2.prop2_1 is
nested
ob2.bar.value = 4; // (const) modified

ob1.prop2 = 4; // (frozen) not modified, bar is a key of obj1
ob2.prop2 = 4; // (const) modified

ob1 = {}; // (frozen) ob1 redeclared (ob1's declaration is not frozen)
ob2 = {}; // (const) ob2 not redeclared (used const)
```

We froze `ob1` so all of its first-level hierarchical properties got frozen (that is, cannot be modified). A frozen object will not throw an error when attempted to be modified, but rather it'll simply ignore the modification done.

However, as we go deeper, you'll observe that `ob1.bar.value` got modified because it's 2 levels down and is not frozen. So, you'll need to recursively freeze nested objects in order to make them *constant*.

Finally, if we look at the last two lines, you'll realize when to use `Object.freeze` and when to use `const`. The `const` declaration is not declared again, whereas `ob1` is redeclared because it's not constant (it's `var`). `Object.freeze` does not freeze the original variable binding and hence is not a replacement for `const`. Similarly, `const` does not freeze properties and is not a replacement for `Object.freeze`.

Also, once an object is frozen, you can no longer add properties to it. However, you can add properties to nested objects (if present).

Default parameter values

In JavaScript, there is no defined way to assign default values to function parameters that are not passed. So programmers usually check for parameters with the `undefined` value (as it is the default value for missing parameters) and assign the default values to them. The following example demonstrates how to do this:

```
function myFunction(x, y, z) {
x = x === undefined ? 1 : x;
y = y === undefined ? 2 : y;
z = z === undefined ? 3 : z;
console.log(x, y, z); //Output "6 7 3"
}
myFunction(6, 7);
```

This can be done in an easier way by providing a default value to function arguments. Here is the code that demonstrates how to do this:

```
function myFunction(x = 1, y = 2, z = 3) {
 console.log(x, y, z);
}
myFunction(6,7); // Outputs 6 7 3
```

In the preceding code block, since we've passed first two arguments in the function calling statement, the default values (that is `x = 1` and `y = 2`) will be overwritten with our passed values (that is `x = 6` and `y = 7`). The third argument is not passed, hence its default value (that is `z =3`) is used.

Also, passing `undefined` is considered as missing an argument. The following example demonstrates this:

```
function myFunction(x = 1, y = 2, z = 3) {
  console.log(x, y, z); // Outputs "1 7 9"
}
myFunction(undefined,7,9);
```

A similar thing happens here. If you want to omit the first argument, just pass `undefined` in that.

Defaults can also be expressions. The following example demonstrates this:

```
function myFunction(x = 1, y = 2, z = x + y) {
  console.log(x, y, z); // Output "6 7 13"
}
myFunction(6,7);
```

Here, we're making use of the argument variables themselves inside a default argument value! That is, whatever you pass as the first two arguments, if the third argument is not passed it'll take the value of the sum of the first two arguments. Since we passed `6` and `7` to the first and second argument, `z` becomes *6 + 7 = 13*.

The spread operator

A **spread operator** is represented by the `...` token. A spread operator splits an iterable object into its individual values.

An **iterable** is an object that contains a group of values and implements the ES6 iterable protocol to let us iterate through its values. An **array** is an example of a built-in iterable object.

A spread operator can be placed wherever multiple function arguments or multiple elements (for array literals) are expected in code.

The spread operator is commonly used to spread the values of an iterable object into the arguments of a function. Let's take the example of an array and see how to split it into the arguments of a function.

To provide the values of an array as a function argument, you can use the `apply()` method of `Function`. This method is available to every function. The following example demonstrates:

```
function myFunction(a, b) {
  return a + b;
}
var data = [1, 4];
var result = myFunction.apply(null, data);
console.log(result); //Output "5"
```

Here, the `apply` method takes an array, extracts the values, passes them as individual arguments to the function, and then calls it.

Here's an example using the modern way, that is, with the spread operator:

```
function myFunction(a, b) {
    return a + b;
}
let data = [1, 4];
let result = myFunction(...data);
console.log(result); //Output "5"
```

During runtime, before the JavaScript interpreter calls the `myFunction` function, it replaces `...data` with the `1,4` expression:

```
let result = myFunction(...data);
```

The previous code is replaced with:

```
let result = myFunction(1,4);
```

After this, the function is called.

Other uses of the spread operator

The spread operator is not just limited to spreading an iterable object into function arguments, but it can be used wherever multiple elements (for example, array literals) are expected in code. So it has many uses. Let's see some other use cases of the spread operator for arrays.

Making array values a part of another array

The spread operator can also be used to make array values a part of another array. The following example code that demonstrates how to make the values of an existing array a part of another array while creating it:

```
let array1 = [2,3,4];
let array2 = [1, ...array1, 5, 6, 7];
console.log(array2); //Output "1, 2, 3, 4, 5, 6, 7"
```

Consider the following code:

```
let array2 = [1, ...array1, 5, 6, 7];
```

This previous code is equivalent to:

```
let array2 = [1, 2, 3, 4, 5, 6, 7];
```

Pushing the values of an array into another array

Sometimes, we may need to push the values of an existing array into the end of another existing array.
This is how programmers used to do it:

```
var array1 = [2,3,4];
var array2 = [1];
Array.prototype.push.apply(array2, array1);
console.log(array2); //Output "1, 2, 3, 4"
```

But from ES6 onward we have a much cleaner way to do it, which is as follows:

```
let array1 = [2,3,4];
let array2 = [1];
array2.push(...array1);
console.log(array2); //Output "1, 2, 3, 4"
```

Here the `push` method takes a series of variables and adds them to the end of the array on which it is called.
See the following line:

```
array2.push(...array1);
```

This will be replaced with the following line:

```
array2.push(2, 3, 4);
```

Spreading multiple arrays

Multiple arrays can be spread on a single-line expression. For example, take the following code:

```
let array1 = [1];
let array2 = [2];
let array3 = [...array1, ...array2, ...[3, 4]];//multi arrayspread
let array4 = [5];
function myFunction(a, b, c, d, e) {
  return a+b+c+d+e;
}
let result = myFunction(...array3, ...array4); //multi array spread
console.log(result); //Output "15"
```

The rest parameter

The **rest parameter** is also represented by the `...` token. The last parameter of a function with `...` is called a rest parameter. The rest parameter is an array type and contains the rest of the parameters of a function when the number of arguments exceeds the number of named parameters.
The rest parameter is used to capture a variable number of function arguments from within a function.
The `arguments` object can also be used to access all arguments passed. The `argument` object is not strictly an array, but it provides some interfaces that are similar to an array.
The following example code shows how to use the `arguments` object to retrieve the extra arguments:

```
function myFunction(a, b) {
    const args = Array.prototype.slice.call(arguments, myFunction.length);
    console.log(args);
}
myFunction(1, 2, 3, 4, 5); //Output "3, 4, 5"
```

This can be done in a much easier and cleaner way, by using the rest parameter. The following example demonstrates to use the rest parameter:

```
function myFunction(a, b, ...args) {
    console.log(args); //Output "3, 4, 5"
}
myFunction(1, 2, 3, 4, 5);
```

The `arguments` object is not an array object. Therefore, to do array operations on the `arguments` object, you need to convert it to an array. The rest parameter is easy to work with.

What is the `...` token called?
The `...` token is called the spread operator or rest parameter, depending on where and how it's used.

Hoisting

Hoisting is JavaScript's default behavior: moving declarations to the top. That means the following code will work in JavaScript:

```
bookName("ES8 Concepts");
function bookName(name) {
   console.log("I'm reading " + name);
}
```

If you're coming from a C/C++ background, this might seem a little weird at first because those languages do not allow you to call a function before at least declaring its prototype. But JavaScript, behind the scenes, hoists the function, that is, all function declarations are moved to the top of the context. So, essentially, the preceding code is the same as the following:

```
function bookName(name) {
   console.log("I'm reading " + name);
}

bookName("ES8 Concepts");
```

Hoisting only moves the declarations to the top, not the initializations. Therefore, although the preceding code works, the following code won't work:

```
bookName("ES8 Concepts"); // bookName is not a function
var bookName = function(name) {
   console.log("I'm reading " + name);
}
```

This is because, as we said earlier, only declarations are hoisted. Therefore, what a browser sees is something like this:

```
var bookName; // hoisted above
bookName("ES8 Concepts"); // bookName is not function
                          // because bookName is undefined
bookName = function(name) { // initalization is not hoisted
   console.log("I'm reading " + name);
}
```

Guess the output of the following code:

```
function foo(a) {
   a();
   function a() {
      console.log("Mehul");
   }
}

foo(); // ??
foo( undefined ); // ??
foo( function(){ console.log("Not Mehul"); } ); // ??
```

Ready to find out? Your possible answers are:

- **`Mehul`**
  `undefined`
  `Not Mehul`
- **`Program throws error`**
- **`Mehul`**
  `Mehul`
  `Mehul`

The output will be :

```
Mehul
Mehul
Mehul
```

Why? Because this is how your browser see this code (after applying the hoisting thing):

```
function foo(a) {
   // the moment below function is declared,
   //the argument 'a' passed is overwritten.
   function a() {
      console.log("Mehul");
   }
   a();
}

foo();
foo( undefined );
foo( function(){ console.log("Not Mehul"); } );
```

Once the function is hoisted, it doesn't matter what you pass in that function. It is always overwritten with the function defined inside the `foo` function.

Therefore, the output is just `Mehul` written three times.

Destructuring assignments

A **destructuring assignment** is an expression that allows you to assign the values or properties of an iterable or object to variables, using a syntax that looks similar to the array or object construction literals respectively.

A destructuring assignment makes it easy to extract data from iterables or objects by providing a shorter syntax. A destructuring assignment is already present in programming languages such as Perl and Python, and works the same way everywhere.

There are two kinds of destructuring assignment expressions: **array** and **object**. Let's see each of them in detail.

The array destructuring assignment

An **array destructuring assignment** is used to extract the values of an iterable object and assign them to the variables. It's called an array destructuring assignment because the expression is similar to an array construction literal.

Programmers used to do it this way to assign the values of an array to the variables:

```
var myArray = [1, 2, 3];
var a = myArray[0];
var b = myArray[1];
var c = myArray[2];
```

Here, we are extracting the values of an array and assigning them to the `a`, `b`, `c` variables respectively.

With an array destructuring assignment we can do this in a one-line statement:

```
let myArray = [1, 2, 3];
let a, b, c;
[a, b, c] = myArray; //array destructuring assignment syntax
```

As you can see, `[a,  b,  c]` is an array destructuring expression.

On the left-hand side of the array destructuring statement, we need to place the variables to which we want to assign the array values, using a syntax similar to an array literal. On the right-hand side, we need to place an array (actually any iterable object) whose values we want to extract.

The previous example code can be made even shorter in this way:

```
let [a, b, c] = [1, 2, 3];
```

Here, we create the variables on the same statement, and instead of providing the array variable, we provide the array with a construction literal.

If there are fewer variables than items in the array, then only the first items are considered.

If you place a non-iterable object on the right-hand side of the array destructuring assignment syntax, then a TypeError exception is thrown.

Ignoring values

We can also ignore some of the values of the iterable. Here is example code that shows how to do this:

```
let [a, , b] = [1, 2, 3]; // notice -->, ,<-- (2 commas)
console.log(a);
console.log(b);
```

The output is as follows:

```
1 3
```

Using the rest operator in an array destructuring assignment

We can prefix the last variable of an array destructuring expression using the `...` token. In this case, the variable is always converted into an array object that holds the rest of the values of the iterable object, if the number of other variables is less than the values in the iterable object.

Consider this example to understand it:

```
let [a, ...b] = [1, 2, 3, 4, 5, 6];
console.log(a);
console.log(Array.isArray(b));
console.log(b);
```

The output is as follows:

```
1
true
2,3,4,5,6
```

In the previous example code, you can see that the `b` variable is converted into an array, and it holds all the other values of the right-hand side array.

Here the `...` token is called the rest operator.
We can also ignore the values while using the rest operator. The following example demonstrates this:

```
let [a, , ,...b] = [1, 2, 3, 4, 5, 6];
console.log(a);
console.log(b);
```

The output is as follows:

```
1 4,5,6
```

Here, we ignored the `2, 3` values.

Default values for variables

While destructuring, you can also provide default values for the variables if an array index is `undefined`. The following example demonstrates this:

```
let [a, b, c = 3] = [1, 2];
console.log(c); //Output "3"
```

Nested array destructuring

We can also extract the values from a multidimensional array and assign them to variables. The following example demonstrates this:

```
let [a, b, [c, d]] = [1, 2, [3, 4]];
```

Using a destructuring assignment as a parameter

We can also use an array destructuring expression as the function parameter for extracting the values of an iterable object, passed as an argument into the function parameters. The following example demonstrates this:

```
function myFunction([a, b, c = 3]) {
  console.log(a, b, c); //Output "1 2 3"
}
myFunction([1, 2]);
```

Earlier in this chapter, we saw that if we pass `undefined` as an argument to a function call, then JavaScript checks for the default parameter value. So, we can provide a default array here too, which will be used if the argument is `undefined`. The following example demonstrates this:

```
function myFunction([a, b, c = 3] = [1, 2, 3]) {
  console.log(a, b, c);  //Output "1 2 3"
}
 myFunction(undefined);
```

Here, we passed `undefined` as an argument and therefore the default array, which is `[1, 2, 3]`, was used to extract the values.

Object destructuring assignments

An **object destructuring assignment** is used to the extract property values of an object and assign them to the variables.

This is a traditional (and still useful) way of assigning property values to an object:

```
var object = {"name" : "John", "age" : 23};
var name = object.name;
var age = object.age;
```

We can do this in a one-line statement, using the object destructuring assignment:

```
let object = {"name" : "John", "age" : 23};
let name, age;
({name, age} = object); //object destructuring assignment syntax
```

On the left-hand side of the object destructuring statement, we need to place the variables to which we want to assign the object property values using a syntax similar to that of an object literal. On the right-hand side, we need to place an object whose property values we want to extract. The statement is finally closed using the `( )` token.

Here the variable names must be the same as the object property names. If you want to assign different variable names, then you can do it this way:

```
let object = {"name" : "John", "age" : 23};
let x, y;
({name: x, age: y} = object);
```

The previous code can be made even shorter this way:

```
let {name: x, age: y} = {"name" : "John", "age" : 23};
```

Here we are creating the variables and object on the same line. We don't need to close the statement using the `( )` token, as we are creating the variables on the same statement.

Default values for variables

You can also provide default values for the variables if the object property is `undefined` while destructuring. The following example demonstrates this:

```
let {a, b, c = 3} = {a: "1", b: "2"};
console.log(c); //Output "3"
```

Some property names are constructed dynamically using expressions. In this case, to extract the property values, we can use the `[ ]` token to provide the property name with an expression. The following example demonstrates this:

```
let {["first"+"Name"]: x} = { firstName: "Eden" };
console.log(x); //Output "Eden"
```

Destructuring nested objects

We can also extract property values from nested objects, that is, objects within objects. The following example demonstrates this:

```
var {name, otherInfo: {age}} = {name: "Eden", otherInfo: {age:
23}};
console.log(name, age); //Eden 23
```

Using the object destructuring assignment as a parameter

Just like the array destructuring assignment, we can also use the object destructuring assignment as a function parameter. The following example demonstrates this:

```
function myFunction({name = 'Eden', age = 23, profession =
                    "Designer"} = {})   {
  console.log(name, age, profession); // Outputs "John 23 Designer"
}
myFunction({name: "John", age: 23});
```

Here, we passed an empty object as a default parameter value, which will be used as a default object if `undefined` is passed as a function argument.

Arrow functions

An **arrow function** is, at first glance, just a fancy way to create regular JavaScript functions (however, there are some surprises). Using arrow functions, you can create concise one-liner functions that actually work!

The following example demonstrates how to create an arrow function:

```
let circumference = (pi, r) => {
  let ans = 2 * pi * r;
  return ans;
}
let result = circumference(3.141592, 3);
console.log(result); // Outputs 18.849552
```

Here, circumference is a variable, referencing to the anonymous arrow function. The previous code is similar to the following code in ES5:

```
var circumference = function(pi, r) {
  var area = 2 * pi * r;
  return area;
}
var result = circumference(3.141592, 3);
console.log(result); //Output 18.849552
```

If your function contains just a single statement (and you want to return the result of that statement), then you don't have to use the `{}` brackets to wrap the code. This makes it a one-liner. The following example demonstrates this:

```
let circumference = (pi, r) => 2 * pi * r;
let result = circumference(3.141592, 3);
console.log(result); //Output 18.849552
```

When `{}` brackets are not used then the value of the statement in the body is automatically returned. The preceding code is equivalent to the following:

```
let circumference = function(pi, r) { return 2 * pi * r; }
let result = circumference(3.14, 3);
console.log(result); //Output 18.84
```

Also, if there's only a single argument, you can omit the brackets to make the code even shorter. Consider the following example:

```
let areaOfSquare = side => side * side;
let result = areaOfSquare(10);
console.log(result); //Output 100
```

Since there is only one argument, `side`, we can omit the circular brackets for this.

The value of "this" in an arrow function

In arrow functions, the value of the `this` keyword is the same as the value of the `this` keyword of the enclosing scope (the global or function scope, whichever the arrow function is defined inside). That means, instead of referring to the context object (that is, the object inside which the function is a property), which is the value of `this` in traditional functions, `this` instead refers to global or function scope, in which the function is called.
Consider this example to understand the difference between the traditional functions and the arrow functions, this value:

```
var car = {
  name: 'Bugatti',
  fuel: 0,
  // site A
  addFuel: function() {
            // site B
            setInterval(function() {
             // site C
             this.fuel++;
             console.log("The fuel is now " + this.fuel);
            }, 1000)
          }
}
```

What do you think will happen when you call the `car.addFuel()` method? If you guessed `The fuel is now undefined` will appear forever, then you are right! But why?!

When you define the `addFuel` method inside the `function() {}` (above site B), your `this` keyword refers to the current object. However, once you go another level deeper into functions (site C), your `this` now points to that particular function and its prototypes. Hence, you cannot access the parent object's property with the `this` keyword.

How do we fix this? Take a look at these arrow functions!

```
var car = {
  name: 'Bugatti',
  fuel: 0,
  // site A
  addFuel: function() {
            // site B
            setInterval(() => { // notice!
             // site C
             this.fuel++;
             console.log("The fuel is now " + this.fuel);
```

```
            }, 1000)
        }
}
```

Now, inside site C, the `this` keyword refers to the parent object. Hence, we're able to access the `fuel` property using the `this` keyword only.

Other differences between arrow and traditional functions

Arrow functions cannot be used as **object constructors**, that is, the `new` operator cannot be applied to them.

Apart from **syntax**, the **value**, and the `new` operator, everything else is the same between arrow and traditional functions, that is, they are both instances of the `Function` constructor.

Enhanced object literals

Once, JavaScript required developers to write complete function names, property names, even when the function name / property name values matched each other (example: `var a = { obj: obj }`). However, ES6/ES7/ES8 and beyond relaxes this and allows the minification and readability of code in a number of ways. Let us see how.

Defining properties

ES6 brought in a shorter syntax for assigning object properties to the values of variables that have the same name as the properties.

Traditionally, you would've done this:

```
var x = 1, y = 2;
var object = {
 x: x,
 y: y
};
console.log(object.x); //output "1"
```

But now, you can do it this way:

```
let x = 1, y = 2;
let object = { x, y };
console.log(object.x); //output "1"
```

Defining methods

ES6 onwards provides a new syntax for defining the methods on an object. The following example demonstrates the new syntax:

```
let object = {
    myFunction(){
        console.log("Hello World!!!"); //Output "Hello World!!!"
    }
}
object.myFunction();
```

This concise function allows the use of `super` in them, whereas traditional object methods don't allow the use of `super`. We will learn more about this later in the book.

Computed property names

Property names that are evaluated during runtime are called computed property names. An expression is usually resolved to find the property name dynamically.
Computed properties were once defined in this way:

```
var object = {};
object["first"+"Name"] = "Eden";//"firstName" is the property name
//extract
console.log(object["first"+"Name"]); //Output "Eden"
```

Here, after creating the object, we attach the properties to the object. But in ES6, we can add the properties with the computed name while creating the object. The following example demonstrates this:

```
let object = {
["first" + "Name"]: "Eden",
};
//extract
console.log(object["first" + "Name"]); //Output "Eden"
```

Trailing commas and JavaScript

Trailing commas are those commas found at the end of an array list, object, or function arguments. They can be useful when adding new elements, parameters, or properties to JavaScript code. It just makes it a little more convenient for developers that they can choose to write an array as `[1,2,3]` or `[1,2,3,]` (notice the comma in the second example)

JavaScript has allowed trailing commas in arrays and objects for a long time. Finally, in ECMAScript 2017 (ES8), the standard now allows you to add trailing commas to function parameters as well.

That means all the following examples are valid JavaScript code:

Arrays:

```
var arr = [1, 2, 3,,,];
arr.length; // 5
arr[3]; // undefined

var arr2 = [1, 2, 3,];
arr2.length; // 3
```

The preceding example is clearly valid JavaScript code and `arr` is created as `[1, 2, 3, undefined, undefined]`

Let us now explore how objects behave with trailing commas.

Objects:

```
var book = {
  name: "Learning ES8",
  chapter: "1",
  reader: "awesome", // trailing comma allowed here
};
```

It can be seen that the code does not throw any error even after putting a comma after the last property name. Let's move on to functions now.

Functions:

```
function myFunc(arg) {
   console.log(arg);
}

function myFunc2(arg,) {
   console.log(arg)
```

```
}

let myFunc3 = (arg) => {
   console.log(arg);
};

let myFunc4 = (arg,) => {
   console.log(arg);
}
```

All the aforementioned function definitions are valid from the ES2017 (ES8) spec.

The semicolon dilemma

You must've seen a lot of JavaScript code with semicolons, and a lot without semicolons as well. And surprisingly, both work fine! While languages such as C, C++, Java, and so on are strict about the use of semicolons, and on the other hand languages such as Python are strict about not using semicolons (only indentations), there is no such fixed rule for JavaScript.

So let's see when is semicolon required in JavaScript.

Automatic semicolon insertion in JavaScript

The ECMAScript Language specification (`http://www.ecma-international.org/ecma-262/5.1/#sec-7.9`) states that:

> *"Certain ECMAScript statements must be terminated with semicolons. Such semicolons may always appear explicitly in the source text"*

But the spec also says:

> *"For convenience, however, such semicolons may be omitted from the source text in certain situations."*

Therefore, the specification states that JavaScript is able to handle automatic semicolon insertion by its own judgment. However, it is extremely error-prone in some cases and not intuitive at all.

Consider this example:

```
var a = 1
var b = 2
var c = 3
```

JavaScript automatically inserts semicolon to make code look like:

```
var a = 1;
var b = 2;
var c = 3;
```

So far so good.

Where to insert semicolons in JavaScript?

At times, you will find yourself skipping semicolons somewhere and you'll see that your code still works! This is strictly opposite to what you find in languages such as C or C++. Let us take a look at a scenario where you can get trapped by not using semicolons properly.

Consider this code:

```
var fn = function (arg) {
    console.log(arg);
} // Semicolon missing

// self invoking function
(function () {
    alert(5);
})() // semicolon missing

fn(7)
```

Take a good look and guess what possible alerts might be, with their orders as well. When you're ready with your answer, look at the following, the code to which JavaScript compiles (not really, just the code after inserting automatic semicolons):

```
var fn = function (arg) {
    alert(arg);
}(function () { // <-- semicolon was missing here,
                // this made it an argument for the function
    alert(5);
})();

fn(7);
```

So instead of invoking that self-invoking function, what you do apparently is, pass that whole function as an argument to the first one. Therefore, try to use semicolons to avoid ambiguity in your code. You can always use JavaScript compressors later on, which will take care of necessary places to leave semicolons intact. The takeaway from here is **use semicolons.**

Summary

In this chapter, we learned about variable scopes, read-only variables, splitting arrays into individual values, passing indefinite parameters to a function, extracting data from objects and arrays, arrow functions, and new syntaxes for creating object properties, hoisting, IIFE, semicolon usage, and more.

In the next chapter, we will learn about built-in objects and symbols, and we will discover tons of fundamental tools JavaScript natively provides us with out-of-the-box.

2
Knowing Your Library

ES6/ES7/ES8 has added lots of new properties and methods to built-in JavaScript objects. These new functionalities aim to help developers avoid using hacks and error-prone techniques to do various operations related to numbers, strings, and arrays.

From the last chapter, you now know a decent amount of background details about JavaScript, how it works, its fundamentals, and basic stuff such as hoisting, scoping variables, and immutability. Now let's move on and take a look at some topics which you'll end up using practically all the time in your code.

In this chapter, we'll cover:

- The new properties and methods of the `Number`, `Object`, `Math`, and `Array` objects
- Representing numeric constants as binary or octal
- Creating multiline strings and the new methods of the `String` object
- Maps and sets
- Using array buffers and typed arrays
- How to iterate properly over arrays using some built-in methods
- String padding, and more!

Working with numbers

ES6, ES2016 (ES7), and ES2017 (ES8) bring new ways of creating numbers and new properties to the `Number` object to make working with numbers easier. The `Number` object was enhanced greatly in ES6 to make it easier to create mathematically rich applications and prevent the common misconceptions that caused the errors.

The binary notation

Earlier, there was no native way to represent numeric constants as binary. But now, you can prefix numeric constants using the `0b` token to make JavaScript interpret them as binary. Here is an example:

```
let a = 0b00001111;
let b = 15;
console.log(a === b);
console.log(a);
```

The output is as follows:

```
true
15
```

Here, `0b00001111` is a binary representation of `15`, base 10 decimal.

The octal notation

The octal notation is a number system where we use only eight digits, that is, from 0 to 7. You can represent a number in octal format with JavaScript if you like.

Earlier, to represent a numeric constant as octal, we needed to prefix the numeric constant using `0`. For example, take a look at the following:

```
const a = 017;
const b = 15;
console.log(a === b);
console.log(a);
```

The output is as follows:

```
true
15
```

But often, programmers new to JavaScript, get confused with octal representations and decimal numbers with 0 at the front. For example, they think 017 is the same as 17. Therefore, to remove this confusion, JavaScript now allows us to prefix numeric constants using 0O to make JavaScript interpret them as octal.
Here is an example to demonstrate this:

```
const a = 0O17;
const b = 15;
console.log(a === b);
console.log(a);
```

The output is as follows:

```
true
15
```

The Number.isInteger(number) method

JavaScript numbers are stored as 64-bit, floating-point numbers. So integers in JavaScript are floating-point numbers without a decimal fraction or a decimal fraction with all 0's.

In ES5, there was no built-in way to check whether a number is an integer or not. There exists a new method to the Number object called isInteger(), which takes a number and returns true or false, depending on whether the number is an integer or not.
Here is an example:

```
let a = 17.0;
let b = 1.2;
console.log(Number.isInteger(a));
console.log(Number.isInteger(b));
```

The output is as follows:

```
true
false
```

The Number.isNaN(value) method

The Number.isNaN function returns true *if and only if* the value equals NaN. Otherwise, in every other case, it returns false. That means it will *not* try to typecast something which is not a number, to a number (which usually results in NaN being returned).

Check the following example:

```
let a = "NaN";
let b = NaN;
let c = "hello";
let d = 12;
console.log(Number.isNaN(a)); // false
console.log(Number.isNaN(b)); // true
console.log(Number.isNaN(c)); // false
console.log(Number.isNaN(d)); // false
```

Here you can see that the `Number.isNaN()` method returns `true` only if the passed value is exactly `NaN`.

You might ask, why not use == or the === operator instead of the `Number.isNaN(value)` method? The `NaN` value is the only value that is not equal to itself, that is, the expression `NaN==NaN` or `NaN===NaN` will return `false`.

If you declare `x = NaN`, then `x` is not equal to itself!

isNaN versus Number.isNaN

To me, a method called `isNaN` should intuitively return `false` only on numbers and `true` on everything else. That is exactly what the `isNaN()` global method does. However, if you're looking to compare a value to `NaN` (which you cannot do with === or ==), then `Number.isNaN` is your choice.

For example:

```
isNaN(' '); // false => because Number(' ') is equal to 0 (a number)
isNaN(true); // false => because Number(true) is equal to 1 (a number)
```

In short, `isNaN` also tries to perform type conversion. That is why some developers consider it broken.

The Number.isFinite(number) method

The global `isFinite()` function takes a value and checks whether it's a finite number or not. But unfortunately, it also returns `true` for values that convert to a `Number` type.

The `Number.isFinite()` method resolves the issue of the `window.isFinite()` function. Here is an example to demonstrate this:

```
console.log(isFinite(10)); // true
console.log(isFinite(NaN)); // false
console.log(isFinite(null)); // true
console.log(isFinite([])); // true
console.log(Number.isFinite(10)); // true
console.log(Number.isFinite(NaN)); // false
console.log(Number.isFinite(null)); // false
console.log(Number.isFinite([])); // false
```

The Number.isSafeInteger(number) method

JavaScript numbers are stored as 64-bit floating-point numbers, following the international IEEE 754 standard. This format stores numbers in 64 bits, where the number (the fraction) is stored in 0 to 51 bits, the exponent in 52 to 62 bits, and the sign in the last bit.
So in JavaScript, safe integers are those numbers that do not need to be rounded to some other integer to fit in with the IEEE 754 representation. Mathematically, numbers from -(2^{53}-1) to (2^{53}-1) are considered as safe integers.
Here is an example to demonstrate this:

```
console.log(Number.isSafeInteger(156));
console.log(Number.isSafeInteger('1212'));
console.log(Number.isSafeInteger(Number.MAX_SAFE_INTEGER));
console.log(Number.isSafeInteger(Number.MAX_SAFE_INTEGER + 1));
console.log(Number.isSafeInteger(Number.MIN_SAFE_INTEGER));
console.log(Number.isSafeInteger(Number.MIN_SAFE_INTEGER - 1));
```

The output is as follows:

```
true
false
true
false
true
false
```

Here, `Number.MAX_SAFE_INTEGER` and `Number.MIN_SAFE_INTEGER` are constant values, introduced in ES6, representing (253-1) and -(253-1) respectively.

The Number.EPSILON property

JavaScript uses binary floating-point representation with the result that computers fail to accurately represent numbers such as 0.1, 0.2, 0.3, and so on. When your code is executed, numbers such as 0.1 are rounded to the nearest number in that format, which results in a small rounding error.
Consider this example:

```
console.log(0.1 + 0.2 == 0.3);
console.log(0.9 - 0.8 == 0.1);
console.log(0.1 + 0.2);
console.log(0.9 - 0.8);
```

The output is as follows:

```
false
false
0.30000000000000004
0.09999999999999998
```

The `Number.EPSILON` property was introduced in ES6, and has a value of approximately 2^{-52}. This value represents a reasonable margin of error when comparing floating-point numbers. Using this number, we can create a custom function to compare floating-point numbers by ignoring the minimal rounding errors. The following example code:

```
function epsilonEqual(a, b) {
  return Math.abs(a - b) < Number.EPSILON;
}
console.log(epsilonEqual(0.1 + 0.2, 0.3));
console.log(epsilonEqual(0.9 - 0.8, 0.1));
```

The output is as follows:

```
true
true
```

Here, `epsilonEqual()` is the custom function that we build to compare whether the two values are equal or not. Now, the output is as expected.

Doing math

ES6 and above add a lot of new methods to the `Math` object, related to trigonometry, arithmetic, and miscellaneous. This lets developers use native methods instead of external math libraries. Native methods are optimized for performance and have better decimal precision.

Trigonometry-related operations

Often there is a need to use mathematical functions related to trigonometry, exponential, logarithmic, and so on. JavaScript provides native methods for that to make our work easy.

The following example code, which shows all trigonometry-related methods that are added to the `Math` object:

```
console.log(Math.sinh(0)); //hyberbolic sine of a value
console.log(Math.cosh(0)); //hyberbolic cosine of a value
console.log(Math.tanh(0)); //hyberbolic tangent of a value
console.log(Math.asinh(0)); //inverse hyperbolic sine of a value
console.log(Math.acosh(1)); //inverse hyperbolic cosine of a value
console.log(Math.atanh(0)); //inverse hyperbolic tangent of a value
console.log(Math.hypot(2, 2, 1));//Pythagoras theorem
```

The output is as follows:

```
0
1
0
0
0
0
3
```

Arithmetic-related operations

Just as we discussed earlier, JavaScript also exposes some functions to perform logarithmic and exponential calculations, which are quite handy in a lot of situations (especially when you're creating games).

The following example code, which shows all arithmetic-related methods added to the `Math` object:

```
console.log(Math.log2(16)); //log base 2
console.log(Math.log10(1000)); //log base 10
console.log(Math.log1p(0)); //same as log(1 + value)
console.log(Math.expm1(0)); //inverse of Math.log1p()
console.log(Math.cbrt(8)); //cube root of a value
```

The output is as follows:

```
4
3
0
0
2
```

Exponential operator

ES7 introduced a new way to perform an exponential calculation with JavaScript, that is, with a new `**` operator. If you're coming from a Python background, you should immediately be able to relate to this. A single asterisk denotes multiplication; however, two together denote an exponential. `a**b` means `a` raised to the power `b`. Take a look at the following example:

```
const a = 5**5;
const b = Math.pow(5, 5);
console.log(a);
console.log(a == b);
```

The output is as follows:

```
3125
true
```

`Math.pow` was earlier used to perform an exponential calculation. Now, `a**b` means multiply `a` `b` times with itself.

Miscellaneous math methods

Apart from the day-to-day math methods and operators we looked at earlier, there are some *boring* methods as well, which are not really used all the time. However, if you're trying to build the next online scientific calculator, here is a list of functions you should be aware of.

The Math.imul(number1, number2) function

The `Math.imul()` function takes two numbers as 32-bit integers and multiplies them. It returns the lower 32 bits of the result. This is the only native way to do 32-bit integer multiplication in JavaScript.
Here is an example to demonstrate this:

```
console.log(Math.imul(590, 5000000)); //32-bit integer multiplication
console.log(590 * 5000000); //64-bit floating-point multiplication
```

The output is as follows:

```
-1344967296
2950000000
```

Here, when multiplication was done, it produced a number so large it couldn't be stored in 32 bits; therefore, the lower bits were lost.

The Math.clz32(number) function

The `Math.clz32()` function returns the number of leading zero bits in the 32-bit representation of a number.
Here is an example to demonstrate this:

```
console.log(Math.clz32(7));
console.log(Math.clz32(1000));
console.log(Math.clz32(295000000));
```

The output is as follows:

```
29
22
3
```

The `Math.clz32()` function is usually used in DSP algorithms to normalize samples in sound and video processing.

The Math.sign(number) function

The `Math.sign()` function returns the sign of a number, indicating whether the number is negative, positive, or zero.
Here is an example to demonstrate this:

```
console.log(Math.sign(11));
console.log(Math.sign(-11));
console.log(Math.sign(0));
```

The output is as follows:

```
1
-1
0
```

From the preceding code, we can see that the `Math.sign()` function returns `1` if the number is positive, `-1` if the number is negative, and `0` if the number is zero.

The Math.trunc(number) function

The `Math.trunc()` function returns the integer part of a number by removing any fractional digit. Here is an example to demonstrate this:

```
console.log(Math.trunc(11.17));
console.log(Math.trunc(-1.112));
```

The output is as follows:

```
11
-1
```

The Math.fround(number) function

The `Math.fround()` function rounds a number to a 32-bit floating point value. Here is an example to demonstrate this:

```
console.log(Math.fround(0));
console.log(Math.fround(1));
console.log(Math.fround(1.137));
console.log(Math.fround(1.5));
```

The output is as follows:

```
0
1
1.1369999647140503
1.5
```

Working with strings

ES6/ES7/ES8 provides new ways of creating strings and adds new properties to the global `String` object and to its instances to make working with strings easier. **Strings** in JavaScript lacked features and capabilities when compared with programming languages such as Python and Ruby; therefore, ES6 enhanced strings to change that.

Before we get into new string features, let's revise JavaScript's internal character encoding and escape sequences. In the Unicode character set, every character is represented by a base 10 decimal number called a code point. A code unit is a fixed number of bits in memory to store a code point. An encoding schema determines the length of code unit. A code unit is 8 bits if the UTF-8 encoding schema is used or 16 bits if the UTF-16 encoding schema is used. If a code point doesn't fit in a code unit, it is split into multiple code units, that is, multiple characters in a sequence representing a single character.

JavaScript interpreters by default interpret JavaScript source code as a sequence of UTF-16 code units. If the source code is written in the UTF-8 encoding schema then there are various ways to tell the JavaScript interpreter to interpret it as a sequence of UTF-8 code units. JavaScript strings are always a sequence of UTF-16 code points.

Any Unicode character with a code point less than 65,536 can be escaped in a JavaScript string or source code using the hexadecimal value of its code point, prefixed with `\u`. Escapes are six characters long. They require exactly four characters following `\u`. If the hexadecimal character code is only one, two, or three characters long, you'll need to pad it with leading zeroes. Here is an example to demonstrate this:

```
const \u0061 = "\u0061\u0062\u0063";
console.log(a); //Output is "abc"
```

The repeat(count) method

The `repeat()` method of a string constructs and returns a new string which contains the specified number of copies on which it was called, concatenated together. Here is an example to demonstrate this:

```
console.log("a".repeat(6)); //Output "aaaaaa"
```

The includes(string, index) method

The `includes()` method is used to find whether one string may be found in another string, returning `true` or `false` as appropriate. Here is an example to demonstrate this:

```
const str = "Hi, I am a JS Developer";
console.log(str.includes("JS")); //Output "true"
```

It takes an optional second parameter representing the position in the string at which to begin searching. Here is an example to demonstrate this:

```
const str = "Hi, I am a JS Developer";
console.log(str.includes("JS", 13)); // Output "false"
```

The startsWith(string, index) method

The `startsWith()` method is used to find whether a string begins with the characters of another string, returning `true` or `false` as appropriate. Here is an example to demonstrate this:

```
const str = "Hi, I am a JS Developer";
console.log(str.startsWith('Hi, I am')); //Output "true"
```

It takes an optional second parameter representing the position in the string at which to begin searching. Here is an example to demonstrate this:

```
const str = "Hi, I am a JS Developer";
console.log(str.startsWith('JS Developer', 11)); //Output "true"
```

The endsWith(string, index) function

The `endsWith()` method is used to find whether a string ends with the characters of another string, returning `true` or `false` as appropriate. It also takes an optional second parameter representing the position in the string that is assumed as the end of the string. Here is an example to demonstrate this:

```
const str = "Hi, I am a JS Developer";
console.log(str.endsWith("JS Developer")); //Output "true"
console.log(str.endsWith("JS", 13)); //Output "true"
```

The indexOf(string) function

Personally, 99% of the time, I use `indexOf` instead of `startsWith` or `endsWith`, `includes` , mainly because I'm very used to it and it's very intuitive. This method will return you the position of your *first occurrence of* a substring passed, in the given string. If not present, it'll return `-1`. For instance:

```
const string = "this is an interesting book and this book is quite good as
well.";
console.log(string.indexOf("this"))

The output for the preceding code is:
0
```

This is because the substring is found at the 0th position of the bigger string. If the substring is not present in the string, `indexOf` returns `-1`.

Can you come up with a replacement for the `startsWith` method in terms of `indexOf`? The following is the answer!

```
const string = "this is a sentence.";
console.log(string.startsWith("this")); // true => starts with "this"
console.log(string.indexOf("this") == 0); // true => starts with "this"
```

The lastIndexOf(string)

The `lastIndexOf` method does pretty much what `indexOf` does, but it will start your search for the substring from the last. So, `indexOf` returns the position of the first occurrence of the substring and `lastIndexOf` returns the last occurrence of the substring:

```
const string = "this is an interesting book and
                this book is quite good as well.";
console.log(string.lastIndexOf("this"))
```

The output from this is:

```
32
```

Although it might be a bit cumbersome to replace the `endsWith` string method with `lastIndexOf`, I still highly recommend you to give it a try and attempt to code it yourself. Once you're ready with your solution, check the following answer:

```
const string = "this is an interesting book and
                this book is quite good as well";
console.log(string.endsWith("well")); // true
console.log(string.lastIndexOf("well") + "well".length == string.length);
// true
```

The padStart(length [, padString])

ES2017 (ES8) provides the `padStart()` method, which pads the given string with another given string to make the original string of the required length. The padding is done from the start of the string.

If no `padString` is passed, spaces are assumed by default. Take a look at the following examples:

```
'normal'.padStart(7);
'1'.padStart(3, '0');
'My Awesome String'.padStart(20, '*');
''.padStart(10, '*');
'Hey!'.padStart(13, 'But this is long');
```

The outputs of each line will be:

```
" normal"
"001"
"****My Awesome String"
"**********"
"But this Hey!"
```

Note that the length supplied in the `padStart` function will be the maximum length of the whole string. If the original string is already larger than the `padStart` supplied length, then no padding is applied at all.

Similarly, as in the last example, if `padString` is longer than the required padding, `padString` is trimmed down, starting from leftmost portion, to the required length.

A possible use case for this could be:

```
for(let i=1;i<=100;i++) {
   console.log(`Test case ${(i+"").padStart(3, "0")}`);
}
```

Can you guess the output for the following? Here's the answer:

```
Test case 001
Test case 002
Test case 003
....
...
Test case 010
Test case 011
...
..
Test case 100
```

This solution is tricky to achieve without the `padStart` function. You'll have to manually keep track of numbers somehow and realize when to append however many numbers of zero. Try to brainstorm an alternate solution without `padStart`.

The padEnd(length [, padString])

`padEnd` is similar to `padStart`. The difference, as the function name says, is that it'll append the supplied padding string to the end of the string.

Consider the following examples again:

```
'normal'.padEnd(7);
'1'.padEnd(3, '0');
'My Awesome String'.padEnd(20, '*');
''.padEnd(10, '*');
'Hey!'.padEnd(13, 'But this is long');
```

The output for this is:

```
"normal "
"100"
"My Awesome String***"
"**********"
"Hey!But this "
```

You can also use `padStart` and `padEnd` together, like:`"1".padStart(5, "*").padEnd(10, "*")`, to produce `****1****`.

Template strings

Template strings are just a new literal for creating strings, which makes various things easier. They provide features such as embedded expressions, multiline strings, string interpolation, string formatting, string tagging, and so on. They are always processed and converted to a normal JavaScript string on runtime; therefore, they can be used wherever we use normal strings.

Template strings are written using backticks instead of single or double quotes. Here is an example of a simple template string:

```
let str1 = `hello!!!`; //template string
let str2 = "hello!!!";
console.log(str1 === str2); //output "true"
```

Expressions

Template strings also bring something called "expressions" to JavaScript. Earlier, there was no other choice than merely concatenating strings together. For example, to embed expressions within normal strings, you would do something like this:

```
var a = 20;
var b = 10;
var c = "JavaScript";
var str = "My age is " + (a + b) + " and I love " + c;
console.log(str);
```

The output is as follows:

```
My age is 30 and I love JavaScript
```

However, now template strings make it much easier to embed expressions in strings. Template strings can contain expressions in them. The expressions are placed in placeholders indicated by a dollar sign and curly brackets, that is, `${expressions}`. The resolved value of expressions in the placeholders and the text between them is passed to a function to resolve the template string to a normal string. The default function just concatenates the parts into a single string. If we use a custom function to process the string parts, then the template string is called a **tagged template string** and the custom function is called a **tag function**.
Here is an example that shows how to embed expressions in a template string:

```
const a = 20;
const b = 10;
const c = "JavaScript";
const str = `My age is ${a+b} and I love ${c}`;
console.log(str);
```

The output is as follows:

```
My age is 30 and I love JavaScript
```

Tagged template literals

Let's create a tagged template string, that is, process the template string literal using a function. Let's implement the tag function to do the same thing as the default function. Here is an example to demonstrate this:

```
const tag = function(strings, aPLUSb, aSTARb) {
  // strings is: ['a+b equals', 'and a*b equals']
  // aPLUSb is: 30
```

```
    // aSTARb is: 200
    return 'SURPRISE!';
};

const a = 20;
const b = 10;

let str = tag `a+b equals ${a+b} and a*b equals ${a*b}`;
console.log(str);
```

The output is as follows:

```
SURPRISE!
```

What just happened? Using a tag function, whatever you return is the final value assigned to the variable. The first argument, strings, contains all the *static* strings in your template literal, as an array. The elements are separated whenever an expression is found. Further arguments are the dynamic values you receive after resolving the expressions inside the template literal.

So, if you modify the `aPLUSb` variable inside the `tag` function, then in the final result the value will be updated. Here's what I mean:

```
const tag = function(strings, aPLUSb, aSTARb) {
  // strings is: ['a+b equals', 'and a*b equals']
  // aPLUSb is: 30
  // aSTARb is: 200
  aPLUSb = 200;
  aSTARb = 30;
  return `a+b equals ${aPLUSb} and a*b equals ${aSTARb}`;
};

const a = 20;
const b = 10;
>
let str = tag `a+b equals ${a+b} and a*b equals ${a*b}`;
console.log(str);
```

Now the output is:

```
a+b equals 200 and a*b equals 30
```

Multiline strings

Template strings provide a new way to create strings that contain multiple lines of text. In ES5, we need to use the `\n` newline character to add new line breaks. Here is an example to demonstrate this:

```
console.log("1\n2\n3");
```

The output is as follows:

```
1
2
3
```

In ES6, using a multiline string, we can simply write:

```
console.log(`1
2
3`);
```

The output is as follows:

```
1
2
3
```

In the preceding code, we simply included new lines where we needed to place `\n`. While converting the template string to the normal string, the new lines are converted to `\n`.

Raw strings

A **raw string** is a normal string in which escaped characters aren't interpreted. We can create a raw string using a template string. We can get a raw version of a template string using the `String.raw` tag function. Here is an example to demonstrate this:

```
let s = String.raw `xy\n${ 1 + 1 }z`;
console.log(s);
```

The output is as follows:

```
xy\n2z
```

Here `\n` is not interpreted as a newline character. Instead, it is a raw string consisting of two characters, that is, `\` and `n`. The length of variable `s` would be `6`. If you create a tagged function and you want to return the raw string, then use the raw property of the first argument.

The raw property is an array that holds raw versions of the strings of the first argument. Here is an example to demonstrate this:

```
let tag = function(strings, ...values) {
  return strings.raw[0]
};
let str = tag `Hello \n World!!!`;
console.log(str);
```

The output is as follows:

```
Hello \n World!!!
```

Escape sequence problem with template literals

Tagged templates are awesome! However, there are certain rules for escape sequences (if used) inside a template literal:

- Anything starting with `\u` will be regarded as a Unicode escape sequence
- Anything starting with `\x` will be regarded as a hexadecimal escape sequence
- Anything starting with `\` and then a digit will be regarded as an octal escape sequence

Therefore, as of now, even with tagged templates, you cannot make use of languages such as LaTeX with template strings because of the syntax of these languages.

LaTeX is a document preparation system usually used to write complicated equations, math formulas, and so on. Using an escape sequence such as `` `E &= \frac{mc^2}{\sqrt{1-\frac{v^2}{c^2}}}` `` would result in a fancy formula:

$$E = \frac{mc^2}{\sqrt{1 - \frac{v^2}{c^2}}}.$$

ES2018 that is the ES9 spec aims to resolve this.

Arrays

There are some new properties added to the global `Array` object and to its instances to make working with arrays easier. Arrays in JavaScript lacked features and capabilities when compared with programming languages such as Python and Ruby. Let's take a look at some popular methods associated with arrays and their use cases.

The Array.from(iterable, mapFunc, this) method

The `Array.from()` method creates a new array instance from an iterable object. The first argument is a reference to the iterable object. The second argument is optional and is a callback (known as the **Map function**) that is called for every element of the iterable object. The third argument is also optional and is the value of this inside the Map function.

Here is an example to demonstrate this:

```
let str = "0123";
let arr = Array.from(str, value => parseInt(value) * 5);
console.log(arr);
```

The output is:

```
[0, 5, 10, 15].
```

`Array.from` would be extremely useful in converting an "array-like" structure to the actual array. For example, when working with the **Document Object Model** (**DOM**) (discussed in `Chapter 10`, *Storage APIs in JavaScript*), quite often, when you get hold of a lot of elements in the DOM tree, you'd like to use methods such as `forEach` on them. However, since methods such as`forEach` only exist for actual arrays, you cannot use them. But, once you convert that to an actual array with the `Array.from` method, you're good to go. A dummy example would be like this:

```
const arr = document.querySelectorAll('div');
/* arr.forEach( item => console.log(item.tagName) ) */ // => wrong
Array.from(arr).forEach( item => console.log(item.tagName) );
// correct
```

`arr.forEach` is wrong, as `arr` is not actually an array. It is "array-like" in structure (more on this later).

The Array.of(values...) method

The `Array.of()` method is an ...) method">alternative to the `Array` constructor for ...) method">creating arrays. When using the `Array` constructor, if we pass only one argument, that too a number, then the `Array` constructor constructs an empty array with the array length property equal to the passed number instead of creating an array of one element with that number in it. Therefore the `Array.of()` method was introduced to resolve this issue.

Here is an example to demonstrate this:

```
let arr1 = Array(2);
let arr2 = Array.of(2);
console.log(arr1);
console.log(arr2);
```

The output is as follows:

```
[undefined, undefined]
[2]
```

You should use `Array.of()` instead of an `Array` constructor when you are constructing a new array instance dynamically, that is when you don't know the type of values and the number of elements.

Instead of browser showing [undefined, undefined], your browser might show [undefined x 2] or [empty x 2] as the output.

The fill(value, startIndex, endIndex) method

The `fill()` method of an array fills all the elements of the array from `startIndex` to `endIndex` (not including `endIndex`) with a given value. Remember that the `startIndex` and `endIndex` arguments are optional; therefore, if they are not provided then the whole array is filled with the given value.

If only `startIndex` is provided then `endIndex` defaults to the length of the array minus 1. If `startIndex` is negative then it's treated as the length of the array plus `startIndex`. If `endIndex` is negative, it is treated as the length of the array plus `endIndex`.

Here is an example to demonstrate this:

```
let arr1 = [1, 2, 3, 4];
let arr2 = [1, 2, 3, 4];
let arr3 = [1, 2, 3, 4];
let arr4 = [1, 2, 3, 4];
let arr5 = [1, 2, 3, 4];
arr1.fill(5);
arr2.fill(5, 1, 2);
arr3.fill(5, 1, 3);
arr4.fill(5, -3, 2);
arr5.fill(5, 0, -2);
console.log(arr1);
console.log(arr2);
console.log(arr3);
console.log(arr4);
console.log(arr5);
```

The output is as follows:

```
[5,5,5,5]
[1,5,3,4]
[1,5,5,4]
[1,5,3,4]
[5,5,3,4]
```

The includes() method

The `includes()` method returns `true` if a certain supplied element exists in an array, and returns `false` if it doesn't exist in that array.

This is simple enough to understand with just an example:

```
const arr = [0, 1, 1, 2, 3, 5, 8, 13];
arr.includes(0); // true
arr.includes(13); // true
arr.includes(21); // false
```

The includes() versus the indexOf() method

Just like for strings, `indexOf` exists for arrays as well and as you expect, it'll return the position of the element in the array. Take a look:

```
const arr = ['apple', 'mango', 'banana'];
console.log(arr.indexOf('apple')); // 0
console.log(arr.indexOf('mango')); // 1
console.log(arr.indexOf('apple') >= 0); // true => apple exists
console.log(arr.includes('apple')); // true => apple exists
console.log(arr.indexOf('pineapple') >= 0); // false => pineapple
                                             // doesn't exists
console.log(arr.includes('pineapple')); // false => pineapple doesn't
                                        //exists
```

So what's the difference? There's not really a difference unless we talk about `NaN` and all that weird stuff. For instance:

```
const arr = ['Some elements I like', NaN, 1337, true, false, 0017];
console.log(arr.includes(NaN)); // true
console.log(arr.indexOf(NaN) >= 0); // false => indexOf says there is
                                    //no NaN element in array
```

This is because, under the hood, `indexOf` uses the equality check (===), which obviously fails on `NaN` , as discussed earlier. Therefore, `includes` is a better choice in the case of arrays.

The find(testingFunc) method

The + method of an array returns an array element if it satisfies the provided testing function. Otherwise, it returns undefined.

The `find()` method takes two arguments; that is, the first argument is the testing function and the second argument is the value of this in the testing function. The second argument is optional.

The testing function has three parameters: the first parameter is the array element being processed, the second parameter is the index of the current element being processed, and the third parameter is the array on which `find()` is called.

The testing function needs to return `true` to satisfy a value. The `find()` method returns the first element which satisfies the provided testing function.

Here is an example to demonstrate the `find()` method:

```
const x = 12;
const arr = [11, 12, 13];
const result = arr.find( (value, index, array) => value == x )
console.log(result); //Output "12"
```

The findIndex(testingFunc) method

The `findIndex()` method is similar to the `find()` method. The `findIndex()` method returns the index of the satisfied array element instead of the element itself. Take a look at this example:

```
const x = 12;
const arr = [11, 12, 13];
const result = arr.findIndex( (value, index, array) => value == x );
console.log(result);
```

The output is `1`.

The copyWithin(targetIndex, startIndex, endIndex) function

The `copyWithin()` method of an array is used to copy the sequence of values of the array to a different position in the array.

The `copyWithin()` method takes three arguments: the first argument represents the target index to which copy elements the second argument represents the index position from which start copying and the third argument represents the index, that is, where copying elements should end.

The third argument is optional and if not provided then it defaults to *length-1,* where length is the length of the array. If `startIndex` is negative then it's calculated as *length+startIndex*. Similarly, if `endIndex` is negative then it's calculated as *length+endIndex*.

Here is an example to demonstrate this:

```
const arr1 = [1, 2, 3, 4, 5];
const arr2 = [1, 2, 3, 4, 5];
const arr3 = [1, 2, 3, 4, 5];
const arr4 = [1, 2, 3, 4, 5];
arr1.copyWithin(1, 2, 4);
```

```
arr2.copyWithin(0, 1);
arr3.copyWithin(1, -2);
arr4.copyWithin(1, -2, -1);
console.log(arr1);
console.log(arr2);
console.log(arr3);
console.log(arr4);
```

The output is as follows:

```
[1,3,4,4,5]
[2,3,4,5,5]
[1,4,5,4,5]
[1,4,3,4,5]
```

The entries(), keys(), and values() methods

The `entries()` method of an array returns an iterable object that contains the key/value pairs for each index of the array. Similarly, the `keys()` method of an array returns an iterable object that contains keys for each of the indexes in the array.

Similarly, the `values()` method of an array returns an iterable object that contains values of the array. The iterable object returned by the `entries()` method stores the key/value pairs in the form of arrays.

The iterable object returned by these functions is not an array.

Here is an example to demonstrate this:

```
const arr = ['a', 'b', 'c'];
const entries = arr.entries();
const keys = arr.keys();
const values = arr.values();
console.log(...entries);
console.log(...keys);
console.log(...values);
```

The output is as follows:

```
0,a 1,b 2,c
0 1 2
a b c
```

`arr.values()` is still very experimental and not implemented in most browsers at the time of writing (November 2017).

Array iteration

You'll find yourself iterating over arrays most of the time during development: arrays from REST APIs, arrays from user input, arrays from here, arrays from there. Therefore, it is essential to get hands-on with some important tools you can use to iterate over arrays.

The map() method

The `map()` method creates and returns a new array and passes every element of that array to the supplied function. Take a look at this example:

```
const arr = [1, 2, 3, 4, 5, 6, 7, 8, 9, 10];
const squaredNums = arr.map( num => num**2 );
console.log(squaredNums);
```

The output is:

```
[1, 4, 9, 16, 25, 36, 49, 64, 81, 100]
```

In the preceding function, when you run `map` on `arr`, every value is passed one by one into the supplied function. The value is contained as `num`. Since we're using the ES6 arrow function notation, everything looks extremely concise and neat.

The filter() method

The `filter()` method creates a new array containing only the elements of a given array which pass a test defined by the programmer.

For example:

```
const arr = ['Mike', 'John', 'Mehul', 'Rahul', 'Akshay', 'Deep','Om',
'Ryan'];
const namesWithOnly4Letters = arr.filter( name => name.length == 4 );
console.log(namesWithOnly4Letters);
```

The output is:

```
["Mike", "John", "Deep", "Ryan"]
```

As you can see, in the filter our supplied function always returns a Boolean. Whenever the inside function returns `true`, that particular element is included in `namesWithOnly4Letters`. Whenever it returns `false`, it is not.

forEach() method

The `forEach()` method calls the given function for every element in the array. It is different from the `map` function because `map` creates a copy of the original array on the basis of what you return from the `map` function. But `foreach` simply runs a function on every element. It doesn't care about what you return from the function.

Take a look at this:

```
const arr = [1, 2, 3, 4];
arr.forEach( (value, index) => console.log(`arr[${index}] = ${value}`) );
```

The output is as follows:

```
arr[0] = 1
arr[1] = 2
arr[2] = 3
arr[3] = 4
```

Clearly, when you want to just do a bunch of operations with the elements of an array, use `forEach`.

some() method

The `some()` method will check if any element in a given array passes a supplied test (with a function). If it finds an element which passes the test, it'll stop there and will not run further (and will return `true`). Otherwise, it'll return `false`.

Here's an example:

```
const arr = [1, 3, 5, 7, 9, 10, 11];
const isAnyElementEven = arr.some( elem => {
   console.log('Checking '+elem);
   return elem % 2 == 0
});
console.log(isAnyElementEven); // true
```

The output is as follows:

```
Checking 1
Checking 3
Checking 5
Checking 7
Checking 9
Checking 10
true
```

Notice that it stops at `10` once the test is passed.

Collections

A **collection** is an object that stores multiple elements as a single unit. ES6 introduced various new collection objects to provide better ways of storing and organizing data.

The array was the only collection object available in ES5. Now we have ArrayBuffers, SharedArrayBuffers, Typed Arrays, Sets, and Maps, which are built in collection objects.

Let's explore the different collection objects provided in JavaScript.

ArrayBuffer

Elements of arrays can be of any type, such as strings, numbers, objects, and so on. Arrays can grow dynamically. The problem with arrays is that they are slow in terms of execution time and occupy more memory. This causes issues while developing applications that require too much computation and deal with plenty of numbers. Therefore array buffers were introduced to tackle this issue.

An **array buffer** is a collection of 8-bit blocks in memory. Every block is an array buffer element. The size of an array buffer needs to be decided while creating it; therefore, it cannot grow dynamically. Array buffers can only store numbers. All blocks are initialized to the number 0 on the creation of an array buffer.

An array buffer object is created using the `ArrayBuffer` constructor:

```
const buffer = new ArrayBuffer(80); //80 bytes size
```

Reading from and writing values into an `ArrayBuffer` object can be done using a `DateView` object. It's not compulsory that only 8 bits are used to represent a number. We can use 8, 16, 32, and 64 bits to represent a number. Here is an example, which shows how to create a `DateView` object and read/write to an `ArrayBuffer` object:

```
const buffer = new ArrayBuffer(80);
const view = new DataView(buffer);
view.setInt32(8,22,false);
const number = view.getInt32(8,false);
console.log(number); //Output "22"
```

Here we created a `DataView` object using the `DataView` constructor. A `DataView` object provides several methods to read and write numbers into an `ArrayBuffer` object. Here we used the `setInt32()` method, which uses 32 bits to store a provided number. All the methods of a `DataView` object that are used to write data to an `ArrayBuffer` object take three arguments. The first argument represents the offset, that is, the byte we want to write the number to. The second argument is the number to be stored. And the third argument is a Boolean type that represents the endian of the number like `false` represents a big-endian.

Similarly, all the methods of a `DataView` object that are used to read data from an `ArrayBuffer` object take two arguments. The first argument is the offset and the second argument represents the endian used.

Here are other functions for storing numbers provided by a `DataView` object:

- `setInt8`: Uses 8 bits to store a number. It takes a signed integer (-ve or +ve).
- `setUint8`: Uses 8 bits to store a number. It takes an unsigned integer (+ve).
- `setInt16`: Uses 16 bits to store a number. It takes a signed integer.
- `setUint16`: Uses 16 bits to store a number. It takes an unsigned integer.
- `setInt32`: Uses 32 bits to store a number. It takes a signed integer.
- `setUint32`: Uses 32 bits to store a number. It takes an unsigned integer.
- `setFloat32`: Uses 32 bits to store a number. It takes a signed decimal number.
- `setFloat64`: Uses 64 bits to store a number. It takes a signed decimal number.

Here are other functions for retrieving stored numbers by a `DataView` object:

- `getInt8`: Reads 8 bits. Returns a signed integer number.
- `getUint8`: Reads 8 bits. Returns an unsigned integer number.
- `getInt16`: Reads 16 bits. Returns a signed integer number.
- `getUint16`: Reads 16 bits. Returns an unsigned integer number.
- `getInt32`: Reads 32 bits. Returns a signed integer number.
- `getUint32`: Reads 32 bits. Returns an unsigned integer number.
- `getFloat32`: Reads 32 bits. Returns a signed decimal number.
- `getFloat64`: Reads 64 bits. Returns a signed decimal number.

Typed arrays

We saw how to read and write numbers in array buffers. But the method was very cumbersome because we had to call a function every time. Typed arrays let us read and write to an `ArrayBuffer` object just like we do for normal arrays.

A **typed array** acts as a wrapper for an `ArrayBuffer` object and treats data from an `ArrayBuffer` object as a sequence of n-bit numbers. The `n` value depends on how we created the typed array.

Next is a code example that demonstrates how to create an `ArrayBuffer` object and read/write to it using a typed array:

```
const buffer = new ArrayBuffer(80);
const typed_array = new Float64Array(buffer);
typed_array[4] = 11;
console.log(typed_array.length);
console.log(typed_array[4]);
```

The output is:

```
10
11
```

Here we created a typed array using the `Float64Array` constructor. It, therefore, treats data in `ArrayBuffer` as a sequence of 64-bit signed decimal numbers. Here the `ArrayBuffer` object size was 640 bits; therefore, only 10 64-bit numbers can be stored.

Similarly, there are other typed array constructors to represent data in `ArrayBuffer` as a sequence of different bit numbers. Here is the list:

- `Int8Array`: Represents 8-bit signed integers
- `Uint8Array`: Represents 8-bit unsigned integers
- `Int16Array`: Represents 16-bit signed integers
- `Uint16Array`: Represents 16-bit unsigned integers
- `Int32Array`: Represents 32-bit signed integers
- `Uint32Array`: Represents 32-bit unsigned integers
- `Float32Array`: Represents 32-bit signed decimal number
- `Float64Array`: Represents 64-bit signed decimal number

Typed arrays provide all the methods that are also provided by normal JavaScript arrays. They also implement the iterable protocol; therefore, they can be used as an iterable object.

We'll need to use typed arrays in Chapter 12 - Shared memory and Atomics

Set

A **Set** is a collection of unique values of any data type. The values in a Set are arranged in insertion order. A Set is created using the `Set` constructor. Here is an example:

```
const set1 = new Set();
const set2 = new Set("Hello!!!");
```

Here `set1` is an empty Set, whereas `set2` was created using values of an iterable object, that is, the characters of a string and the string, was not empty; therefore, `set2` is non-empty. The following example code demonstrates various operations that can be done on a Set:

```
let set = new Set("Hello!!!");
set.add(12); //add 12
console.log(set.has("!")); //check if value exists
console.log(set.size);
set.delete(12); //delete 12
console.log(...set);
set.clear(); //delete all values
```

The output is as follows:

```
true
6
H e l o !
```

Here we added nine items to the `Set` object but the size was only six because the Set automatically deletes duplicate values. The characters `l` and `!` were repeated multiple times. The `Set` object also implements the iterable protocol so they can be used as an iterable object.

Sets are used when you want to maintain a collection of values and check if a value exists instead of retrieving a value. For example, Sets can be used as an alternative to an array if you only use the `indexOf()` method of the array in your code to check if a value exists.

WeakSet

Here are the differences between `Set` and `WeakSet` objects:

- A `Set` can store primitive types and object references whereas a `WeakSet` object can only store object references
- One important features `WeakSet` objects is that if there is no other reference to an object stored in a `WeakSet` object then they are garbage-collected
- Lastly, a `WeakSet` object is not enumerable: that is, you cannot find its size; it also doesn't implement the iterable protocol

Apart from these three differences, `WeakSet` behaves exactly the same way as `Set`. Everything else apart from these three differences is same between a `Set` and `WeakSet` object.

A `WeakSet` object is created using the `WeakSet` constructor. You cannot pass an iterable object as an argument to a `WeakSet` object.

Here is an example to demonstrate `WeakSet`:

```
let weakset = new WeakSet();
(function(){
   let a = {};
   weakset.add(a);
})();  //here 'a' is garbage collected from weakset
console.log(weakset.size); //output "undefined"
console.log(...weakset); //Exception is thrown
weakset.clear(); //Exception, no such function
```

Map

A **Map** is a collection of key/value pairs. Keys and values of a Map can be of any data type. Key/value pairs are arranged in insertion order. A `Map` object is created using the `Map` constructor.

Here is an example, which demonstrates how to create a `Map` object and do various operations on it:

```
let map = new Map();
let o = {n: 1};
map.set(o, "A"); //add
map.set("2", 9);
console.log(map.has("2")); //check if key exists
console.log(map.get(o)); //retrieve value associated with key
console.log(...map);
map.delete("2"); //delete key and associated value
map.clear(); //delete everything
//create a map from iterable object
let map_1 = new Map([[1, 2], [4, 5]]);
console.log(map_1.size); //number of keys
```

The output is as follows:

```
true
A
[object Object],A 2,9
2
```

While creating a `Map` object from an iterable object, we need to make sure that the values returned by the iterable object are arrays, each of length `2`; that is, index `0` is the key and index `1` is the value.

If we try to add a key that already exists then it's overwritten. `Map` objects also implement the iterable protocol and can therefore also be used as an iterable object. While iterating Maps using the iterable protocol, they return arrays with key/value pairs as you can see in the preceding example.

WeakMap

`WeakMap`, as the name suggests, is an object in which keys are weakly referenced to the key/value pairs. That means that values can be anything. The keys are weakly referenced as keys are objects.

Here are the differences between `Map` and `WeakMap` objects:

- Keys of a `Map` object can be of primitive types or object references but keys in a `WeakMap` object can only be object references
- One of the important features of a `WeakMap` object is that if there is no other reference to an object that is referenced by a key then the key is garbage-collected
- Lastly, a `WeakMap` object is not enumerable, that is, you cannot find its size and it doesn't implement the iterable protocol

In every other particular, apart from these three differences `Map` and `WeakMap` objects are similar.

`WeakMap` is created using a `WeakMap` constructor. Here is an example that demonstrates its usage:

```
let weakmap = new WeakMap();

(function(){
  let o = {n: 1};
  weakmap.set(o, "A");
})();  // here 'o' key is garbage collected

let s = {m: 1};
weakmap.set(s, "B");
console.log(weakmap.get(s));
console.log(...weakmap); // exception thrown
weakmap.delete(s);
weakmap.clear(); // Exception, no such function
let weakmap_1 = new WeakMap([[{}, 2], [{}, 5]]); //this works
console.log(weakmap_1.size); //undefined
```

Objects

Objects have existed in JavaScript for a long time. They form the backbone of JavaScript, as almost every data type can be associated with *objects*. (`new String()`, `new Number()`, `new Boolean()`, and so on). You'll often find yourself working and manipulating objects all the time when working with web applications or JavaScript in general.

ES6, ES2016 (ES7), and ES2017 (ES8) introduce a lot of new properties and methods associated with objects. Let us take a look at them.

Object.values()

ES8 introduced the `Object.values()` method so that a programmer can retrieve all the values of an object as an array. This was earlier possible by manually iterating over every property of the object and storing its value in the array.

Here's an example:

```
const obj = {
    book: "Learning ES2017 (ES8)",
    author: "Mehul Mohan",
    publisher: "Packt",
    useful: true
};
console.log(Object.values(obj));
```

The output will be:

```
["Learning ES2017 (ES8)", "Mehul Mohan", "Packt", true]
```

Object.entries()

`Object.entries()` can be used to convert an object into a key/value pair in the form of an array. That means your object will be converted into a 2D array (at the simplest level), with each element being another array containing a key and value. Take a look at this:

```
const obj = {
    book: "Learning ES2017 (ES8)",
    author: "Mehul Mohan",
    publisher: "Packt",
    useful: true
};
```

```
console.log(Object.entries(obj));
```

The output will be:

```
[["book","Learning ES2017 (ES8)"],["author","Mehul
Mohan"],["publisher","Packt"],["useful",true]]
```

The __proto__ property

JavaScript objects have an internal `[[prototype]]` property that references the object's prototype, that is, the object it inherits: the **prototypal inheritance model**, which JavaScript uses. To read the property, we had to use `Object.getPrototypeof()` and to create a new object with a given prototype, we had to use the `Object.create()` method. A `[[prototype]]` property cannot be directly read or be modified.

Inheriting was cumbersome due to the nature of the `[[prototype]]` property; therefore, some browsers added a special `__proto__` property in objects, which is an accessor property that exposes the internal `[[prototype]]` property and makes working with prototypes easier. The `__proto__` property was not standardized in ES5, but due to its popularity, it was standardized in later versions.

Here is an example to demonstrate this:

```
//In ES5
var x = {prop1: 12};
var y = Object.create(x, {prop2: {value: 13}});
console.log(y.prop1); //Output "12"
console.log(y.prop2); //Output "13"
console.log(x); // Output: {prop1: 12}
console.log(y); // Output: {prop2: 13}

//In ES6 onwards
let a = {prop1: 12, __proto__: {prop2: 13}};
console.log(a.prop1); //Output "12"
console.log(a.prop2); //Output "13"
console.log(a); // Output: {prop1: 12}
console.log(a.__proto__); // Output: {prop2: 13}
```

Carefully observe:

- In the ES5 example, object `y` *inherits* from object `x`; therefore, when you simply use `console.log` on the object `y`, the properties it inherits from object `x` are not visible directly (or rather they are hidden). However, when you try to access `y.prop2`, JavaScript doesn't find it on object `y`, so it looks on the `__proto__` chain (which is how JavaScript is built to work) and finds that there is, in fact, a reference available for `prop2` on the proto chain. However, it was not possible to edit that directly in ES5.
- With ES6/ES7/ES8/ES.next and onwards, you can directly add values to the prototype chain of the object.

The Object.is(value1, value2) method

The `Object.is()` method determines whether two values are equal or not. It is similar to the === operator but there are some special cases for the `Object.is()` method. Here is an example that demonstrates special cases:

```
console.log(Object.is(0, -0));
console.log(0 === -0);
console.log(Object.is(NaN, 0/0));
console.log(NaN === 0/0);
console.log(Object.is(NaN, NaN));
console.log(NaN ===NaN);
```

The output is as follows:

```
false
true
true
false
true
false
```

Here's a handy table you might want to look at for the differences between **0**, **==**, **===**, and **Object.is:**

Sameness Comparisons

x	y	==	===	Object.is
undefined	undefined	true	true	true
null	null	true	true	true
true	true	true	true	true
false	false	true	true	true
"foo"	"foo"	true	true	true
{ foo: "bar" }	x	true	true	true
0	0	true	true	true
+0	-0	true	true	false
0	false	true	false	false
""	false	true	false	false
""	0	true	false	false
"0"	0	true	false	false
"17"	17	true	false	false
[1,2]	"1,2"	true	false	false
new String("foo")	"foo"	true	false	false
null	undefined	true	false	false
null	false	false	false	false
undefined	false	false	false	false
{ foo: "bar" }	{ foo: "bar" }	false	false	false
new String("foo")	new String("foo")	false	false	false
0	null	false	false	false
0	NaN	false	false	false
"foo"	NaN	false	false	false
NaN	NaN	false	false	true

While it might seem intuitive that `Object.is` can compare if two given objects are same, that is not the case. `x = {foo: 1}` and `y = {foo: 1}` are *not* same for all three operators (==, ===, and `Object.is`).

The Object.setPrototypeOf(object, prototype) method

The `Object.setPrototypeOf()` method is just another way to assign the `[[prototype]]` property of an object, which we have just discussed. You can either use this method or directly work with the `__proto__` property. However, working with a method is a cleaner and easier-to-read approach. Here is an example to demonstrate this:

```
let x = {x: 12};
let y = {y: 13};
Object.setPrototypeOf(y, x);
console.log(y.x); //Output "12"
console.log(y.y); //Output "13"
```

The Object.assign(targetObj, sourceObjs...) method

The `Object.assign()` method is used is used to ...) method">copy the values of all enumerable own properties from one or more source objects to a target object. This method will return `targetObj`. Here is an example which demonstrates this:

```
let x = {x: 12};
let y = {y: 13, __proto__: x};
let z = {z: 14, get b() {return 2;}, q: {}};
Object.defineProperty(z, "z", {enumerable: false});
let m = {};
Object.assign(m, y, z);
console.log(m.y);
console.log(m.z);
console.log(m.b);
console.log(m.x);
console.log(m.q == z.q);
```

The output is as follows:

```
13
undefined
2
undefined
true
```

Here is a list of important things to keep in mind while using the `Object.assign()` method:

- It invokes getters on the sources and setters on the target.
- It just assigns values of the properties of the source to the new or existing properties of the target.
- It doesn't copy the `[[prototype]]` property of sources.
- JavaScript property names can be strings or symbols. `Object.assign()` copies both.
- Property definitions are not copied from sources; therefore, you need to use `Object.getOwnPropertyDescriptor()` instead.
- It ignores copying keys with null and undefined values.

Object.getOwnPropertyDescriptors()

Introduced in ES8, the `Object.getOwnPropertyDescriptors()` method will return all the property descriptors for a given object. What does that mean exactly? Let's take a look:

```
const details = {
  get food1() { return 'tasty'; },
  get food2() { return 'bad'; }
};
Object.getOwnPropertyDescriptors(details);
```

The output produced is:

```
{
    food1: {
        configurable: true,
        enumerable: true,
        get: function food1(){}, //the getter function
        set: undefined
    },
    food2: {
        configurable: true,
```

```
            enumerable: true,
            get: function food2(){}, //the getter function
            set: undefined
        }
    }
```

The `get()` function fires when you try to access the property (but when you also want to do a bunch of stuff first). So, when you do `details.food1`, `tasty` is returned.

The practical usage of this is mostly in **Decorators** (which is a whole new topic) and creating a shallow clone, as shown here:

```
const x = { foo: 1, __proto__: { bar: 2 } };
const y = Object.create(
  Object.getPrototypeOf(x),
  Object.getOwnPropertyDescriptors(x)
);
console.log(y.__proto__); // { bar: 2 }
```

Summary

In this chapter, we learned about new features added in ES8, ES7, and ES6 for working with numbers, strings, arrays, and objects. We saw how arrays impact performance in math-rich applications and how array buffers can be used instead. We also walked through the new collection objects provided by ES8.

In the next chapter, we will take a look at the Symbols and Iteration protocol, and we will also explore the `yield` keyword and generators. A lot of exciting and cutting-edge stuff is coming your way! Hold tight!

3
Using Iterators

ES8 and earlier versions introduced new object interfaces and loops for iteration. The addition of the new iteration protocols opens up a new world of algorithms and abilities for JavaScript. We will start the chapter by introducing the symbols and various properties of the `Symbol` object. We will also learn how execution stacks are created for the nested function calls, their impacts, and how to optimize their performance and memory usage. Although symbols are a separate topic to iterators, we will still be covering symbols in this chapter, because to implement the iterable protocol, you need to use symbols.
In this chapter, we'll cover:

- Using symbols as the object property keys
- Implementing the iteration protocols in objects
- Creating and using the `generator` object
- Using the `for...of` loop for iterating
- The tail call optimization

Symbols – primitive data type

Symbols are a primitive type that was first introduced in ES6. A symbol is a unique and immutable value. Here is an example that shows how to create a symbol:

```
const s = Symbol();
```

Symbols don't have a literal form; therefore, we need to use the `Symbol()` function to create a symbol. The `Symbol()` function returns a unique symbol every time it is called.

The `Symbol()` function takes an optional string parameter that represents the description of the symbol. A description of a symbol can be used for debugging, but not to access the symbol itself. Two symbols with the same description are not equal at all. Here is an example to demonstrate this:

```
let s1 = Symbol("My Symbol");
let s2 = Symbol("My Symbol");
console.log(s1 === s2); // Outputs false
```

From the preceding example, we can also say that a symbol is a string-like value that can't clash with any other value.

The typeof operator

The `typeof` operator is used to determine the type of value a particular variable/constant is held for `Symbol`, `typeof` outputs `symbol`. Here is an example to demonstrate the same:

```
const s = Symbol();
console.log(typeof s); //Outputs "symbol"
```

Using the `typeof` operator is the only way to identify whether a variable holds a symbol.

The new operator

You cannot apply the `new` operator to the `Symbol()` function. The `Symbol()` function detects whether it's being used as a constructor, and if `true`, it then throws an exception. Here is an example to demonstrate this:

```
try {
  let s = new Symbol(); //"TypeError" exception
}
catch(e) {
  console.log(e.message); //Output "Symbol is not a constructor"
}
```

But the JavaScript engine can use the `Symbol()` function internally as a constructor to wrap a symbol in an object. Therefore, `s` will be equal to object(s).

All primitive types introduced from ES6 onward will not allow their constructors to be invoked manually.

Using symbols as the object property keys

Until ES5, the JavaScript object property keys had to be string type. But since ES6, the JavaScript object property keys can be strings or symbols. Here is an example that demonstrates how to use a symbol as an object property key:

```
let obj = null;
let s1 = null;
(function(){
 let s2 = Symbol();
 s1 = s2;
 obj = {[s2]: "mySymbol"}
 console.log(obj[s2]);
 console.log(obj[s2] == obj[s1]);
})();
console.log(obj[s1]);
```

The output is:

```
mySymbol
true
mySymbol
```

From the preceding code, you can see that in order to create or retrieve a property key using symbols, you need to use the `[]` token. We saw the `[]` token while discussing the computed property names in `Chapter 2`, *Knowing Your Library*.

To access a symbol property key, we need the symbol. In the previous example, both `s1` and `s2` hold the same symbol value.

The Object.getOwnPropertySymbols() method

The `Object.getOwnPropertyNames()` method cannot retrieve the symbol properties. Therefore, ES6 introduced `Object.getOwnPropertySymbols()` to retrieve an array of symbol properties of an object. Here is an example to demonstrate this:

```
let obj = {a: 12};
let s1 = Symbol("mySymbol");
let s2 = Symbol("mySymbol");
Object.defineProperty(obj, s1, {
enumerable: false
});
obj[s2] = "";
console.log(Object.getOwnPropertySymbols(obj));
```

The output is as follows:

```
Symbol(mySymbol),Symbol(mySymbol)
```

From the previous example, you can see that the `Object.getOwnPropertySymbols()` method can also retrieve the non-enumerable symbol properties.

The `in` operator can find the symbol properties in an object, whereas the `for...in` loop and `Object.getOwnPropertyNames()` cannot find the symbol properties in an object for the sake of backward compatibility.

The Symbol.for(string) method

The `Symbol` object maintains a registry of the key/value pairs, where the key is the symbol description, and the value is the symbol. Whenever we create a symbol using the `Symbol.for()` method, it gets added to the registry and the method returns the symbol. If we try to create a symbol with a description that already exists, then the existing symbol will be retrieved.

The advantage of using the `Symbol.for()` method instead of the `Symbol()` method to create symbols is that while using the `Symbol.for()` method, you don't have to worry about making the symbol available globally, because it's always available globally. Here is an example to demonstrate this:

```
let obj = {};
(function(){
 let s1 = Symbol("name");
 obj[s1] = "Eden";
})();
//obj[s1] cannot be accessed here
(function(){
 let s2 = Symbol.for("age");
 obj[s2] = 27;
})();
console.log(obj[Symbol.for("age")]); //Output "27"
```

Well-known symbols

In addition to your own symbols, ES6 comes up with a built-in set of symbols, known as well-known symbols. Here is a list of properties, referencing some important built-in symbols:

- `Symbol.iterator`
- `Symbol.match`
- `Symbol.search`
- `Symbol.replace`
- `Symbol.split`
- `Symbol.hasInstanceSymbol.species`
- `Symbol.unscopables`
- `Symbol.isContcatSpreadable`
- `Symbol.toPrimitive`

You will come across the use of these symbols in various chapters of this book.

When referring to the well-known symbols in the text, we usually prefix them using the `@@` notation. For example, the `Symbol.iterator` symbol is referred to as the `@@iterator` method. This is done to make it easier to refer to these symbols in the text.

The iteration protocol

An iteration protocol is a set of rules that an object needs to follow for implementing the interface. When this protocol is used, a loop or a construct can iterate over a group of values of the object.

JavaScript has two iteration protocols known as the **iterator protocol** and the **iterable protocol**.

The iterator protocol

Any object that implements the iterator protocol is known as an **iterator**. According to the iterator protocol, an object needs to provide a `next()` method that returns the next item in the sequence of a group of items.
Here is an example to demonstrate this:

```
let obj = {
 array: [1, 2, 3, 4, 5],
 nextIndex: 0,
 next: function() {
         return this.nextIndex < this.array.length ? {value:
this.array[this.nextIndex++], done: false} : {done: true}
       }
};
console.log(obj.next().value);
console.log(obj.next().value);
console.log(obj.next().value);
console.log(obj.next().value);
console.log(obj.next().value);
console.log(obj.next().done);
```

The output is as follows:

```
1
2
3
4
5
true
```

If you look closely, you'll realize that the `next` method inside the `obj` object is as follows:

```
return this.nextIndex < this.array.length ? {value:
this.array[this.nextIndex++], done: false} : {done: true}
```

This can be written as follows:

```
if(this.nextIndex < this.array.length) {
  this.nextIndex++;
  return { value: this.array[this.nextIndex], done: false }
} else {
  return { done: true }
}
```

This clearly tells us that we'll increment `nextIndex` and send the next element from the `array` in the object `obj` if a new element exists there. When there's no element left, we return `{ done: true }`.

The iterable protocol

Any object that implements the **iterable protocol** is known as an iterable. According to the iterable protocol, an object needs to provide the `@@iterator` method; that is, it must have the `Symbol.iterator` symbol as a property key. The `@@iterator` method must return an iterator object.
Here is an example to demonstrate this:

```
let obj = {
  array: [1, 2, 3, 4, 5],
  nextIndex: 0,
  [Symbol.iterator]: function(){
    return {
     array: this.array,
     nextIndex: this.nextIndex,
     next: function(){
       return this.nextIndex < this.array.length ?
          {value: this.array[this.nextIndex++], done: false} :
          {done: true};
     }
    }
  }
};
let iterable = obj[Symbol.iterator]()
console.log(iterable.next().value);
console.log(iterable.next().value);
console.log(iterable.next().value);
console.log(iterable.next().value);
console.log(iterable.next().value);
console.log(iterable.next().done);
```

The output is as follows:

```
1
2
3
4
5
true
```

This is all well and good, but what is the use of doing it?

The preceding two code blocks show you how to implement the iterable protocol on your own. However, things such as **arrays** come with the iterable protocol (that is, their `__proto__` chain implements the `Symbol.iterator` method), which is implemented by default thus saving a developer's time. Let's take a look at an example:

```
const arr = [1, 2]
const iterator = arr[Symbol.iterator](); // returns you an iterator
console.log(iterator.next())
console.log(iterator.next())
console.log(iterator.next())
```

Based on what we've learned so far, what do you think the output should be?

The output is as follows:

```
{ value: 1, done: false }
{ value: 2, done: false }
{ value: undefined, done: true }
```

Let us now take a look at generators, which are more or less, similar to iterators.

Generator function

A `generator` is a normal function, but instead of returning a single value, it returns multiple values one by one. Calling a `generator` function doesn't execute its body immediately, but rather returns a new instance of the `generator` object (that is, an object that implements both, iterable and iterator protocols).

Every `generator` object holds a new execution context of the `generator` function. When we execute the `next()` method of the `generator` object, it executes the `generator` function's body until the `yield` keyword is encountered. It returns the yielded value and pauses the function. When the `next()` method is called again, it resumes the execution and then returns the next yielded value. The `done` property is `true` when the `generator` function doesn't yield any value.

A `generator` function is written using the `function*` expression. Here is an example to demonstrate this:

```
function* generator_function(){
  yield 1;
  yield 2;
  yield 3;
  yield 4;
  yield 5;
}
let generator = generator_function();
console.log(generator.next().value);
console.log(generator.next().value);
console.log(generator.next().value);
console.log(generator.next().value);
console.log(generator.next().value);
console.log(generator.next().done);

generator = generator_function();

let iterable = generator[Symbol.iterator]();
console.log(iterable.next().value);
console.log(iterable.next().value);
console.log(iterable.next().value);
console.log(iterable.next().value);
console.log(iterable.next().value);
console.log(iterable.next().done);
```

The output is as follows:

```
1
2
3
4
5
true
1
2
3
4
5
true
```

There is an expression following the `yield` keyword. The value of the expression is what is returned by the `generator` function via the iterable protocol. If we omit the expression, then `undefined` is returned. The value of the expression is what we call, the yielded value.

We can also pass an optional argument to the `next()` method. This argument becomes the value returned by the `yield` statement, where the `generator` function is currently paused. Here is an example to demonstrate this:

```
function* generator_function(){
  const a = yield 12;
  const b = yield a + 1;
  const c = yield b + 2;
  yield c + 3; // Final Line
}
const generator = generator_function();
console.log(generator.next().value);
console.log(generator.next(5).value);
console.log(generator.next(11).value);
console.log(generator.next(78).value);
console.log(generator.next().done);
```

The output is as follows:

```
12
6
13
81
true
```

Here's the explanation of this output:

1. On the first `generator.next()` call, `yield 12` is called and the value `12` is returned.
2. On the second `generator.next(5)` call, the previous yield (which was stored in `const a`) gets the passed value (that is, `5`), and then the second yield (`a + 1`). Then, `yield 5 + 1` is called and the value `6` is returned (careful: `a` is not `12` here).
3. On the third `generator.next(11)` call, `const b` becomes `11`, and then because it's the sum of *11 + 2*, `13` is yielded.
4. This is followed till the last process, that is, until the line `Final Line`, as mentioned in the example.
5. As `yield` finally returns a value and its `done` status, after executing `yield c + 3`, there is apparently no value to yield. Hence, the value returned is `undefined` and `done` is `true`.

The return(value) method

You can end a generator function any time before it has yielded all the values by using the return() method of the generator object. The return() method takes an optional argument, representing the final value to return.

Here is an example demonstrating this:

```
function* generator_function(){
 yield 1;
 yield 2;
 yield 3;
}
const generator = generator_function();
console.log(generator.next().value);
console.log(generator.return(22).value);
console.log(generator.next().done);
```

The output is as follows:

```
1
22
true
```

The throw(exception) method

You can manually trigger an exception inside a generator function using the throw() method of the generator object. You must pass an exception to the throw() method that you want to throw. Here is an example to demonstrate this:

```
function* generator_function(){
try {
 yield 1;
} catch(e) {
 console.log("1st Exception");
}
try {
 yield 2;
} catch(e) {
 console.log("2nd Exception");
}
}
const generator = generator_function();
console.log(generator.next().value);
console.log(generator.throw("exception string").value);
```

```
console.log(generator.throw("exception string").done);
```

The output is as follows:

```
1
1st Exception
2
2nd Exception
true
```

In the preceding example, you can see that the exception is thrown where the function was last paused. After the exception is handled, the `throw()` method continues execution, and returns the next yielded value.

The yield* keyword

The `yield*` keyword inside a `generator` function takes an iterable object as the expression and iterates it to yield its values. Here is an example to demonstrate this:

```
function* generator_function_1(){
 yield 2;
 yield 3;
}
function* generator_function_2(){
 yield 1;
 yield* generator_function_1();
 yield* [4, 5];
}
const generator = generator_function_2();
console.log(generator.next().value);
console.log(generator.next().value);
console.log(generator.next().value);
console.log(generator.next().value);
console.log(generator.next().value);
console.log(generator.next().done);
```

The output is as follows:

```
1
2
3
4
5
true
```

The for...of loop

Until now, we have been iterating over an iterable object using the `next()` method, which is a cumbersome task. ES6 introduced the `for...of` loop to make this easier.

The `for...of` loop was introduced to iterate over the values of an iterable object. Here is an example to demonstrate this:

```
function* generator_function(){
 yield 1;
 yield 2;
 yield 3;
 yield 4;
 yield 5;
}
let arr = [1, 2, 3];
for(let value of generator_function()){
 console.log(value);
}
for(let value of arr){
 console.log(value);
}
```

The output is as follows:

```
1
2
3
4
5
1
2
3
```

Tail call optimization

Whenever a function call is made, an execution stack is created in the stack memory to store the variables of the function. **Tail call optimization** basically means that you reuse the allocated stack in memory if there's no information in that stack that is required later in the code execution sequence.

Why tail call optimization?

When a function call is made inside another function call, a new execution stack is created for the inner function call. However, the problem is that the inner function execution stack takes up some extra memory--that is, it stores an extra address, representing where to resume the execution when this function finishes executing. Switching and creating the execution stacks also takes some additional CPU time. This problem is not noticeable when there are a couple of hundred, nested levels of calls, but it's noticeable when there are thousands or more nested levels of calls--that is, the JavaScript engines throw the `RangeError: Maximum call stack size exceeded` exception. You might have, at some point, experienced the `RangeError` exception while creating a recursive function.

A tail call is a function call that is performed optionally at the very end of a function with the `return` statement. If a tail call leads to the same function call again and again, then it's called a **tail-recursion**, which is a special case of recursion. What's special about tail calls is that there is a way to actually prevent the extra CPU-time and memory usage while making the tail calls, and that is by reusing the stack of the out function, instead of creating a new execution stack. Reusing the execution stack while making a tail call is called tail call optimization.

JavaScript supports tail call optimization in specific browsers if the script is written in the `"use strict"` mode. Let's see an example of a tail call:

```
"use strict";
function _add(x, y){
    return x + y;
}
function add1(x, y){
    x = parseInt(x);
    y = parseInt(y); //tail call
    return _add(x, y);
}
function add2(x, y) {
    x = parseInt(x);
    y = parseInt(y);
    //not tail call
    return 0 + _add(x, y);
}
console.log(add1(1, '1')); //2
console.log(add2(1, '2')); //3
```

Here, the `_add()` call in the `add1()` function is a tail call, as it's the final action of the `add1()` function. However, the `_add()` call in the `add2()` function is not a tail call, as it's not the final act; adding `0` to the result of `_add()` is the final act.

The `_add()` call in `add1()` doesn't create a new execution stack. Instead, it reuses the `add1()` function's execution stack; in other words, the tail call optimization occurs.

Tail call optimization spec is **not actively** being developed for Chrome and is only implemented in Safari as of now. Hence, you can only use TCO in Safari.

Converting non-tail calls into tail calls

As tail calls are optimized, you must use tail calls whenever possible, instead of non-tail calls. You can optimize your code by converting the non-tail calls into tail calls.
Let's see an example of this, which is similar to the previous one:

```
"use strict";
function _add(x, y) {
    return x + y;
}

function add(x, y) {
 x = parseInt(x);
 y = parseInt(y);
 const result = _add(x, y);
 return result;
}

console.log(add(1, '1'));
```

In the previous code, the `_add()` call was not a tail call, and therefore, two execution stacks were created. We can convert it into a tail call in this way:

```
function add(x, y){
    x = parseInt(x);
    y = parseInt(y);
    return _add(x, y);
}
```

Here, we omitted the use of the `result` variable and instead lined up the function call with the `return` statement. There are many other similar strategies to convert non-tail calls into tail calls.

Summary

In this chapter, we learned a new way of creating the object property keys using symbols. We saw the iterator and iterable protocols and learned how to implement these protocols in custom objects. Then, we learned how to iterate over an iterable object using the `for...of` loop. Finally, we ended the chapter by learning what tail calls are, and how they are optimized.

In the next chapter, we will learn about how to do asynchronous programming with Promises and the recently launched async/await feature in ES8, which makes asynchronous code look much more like synchronous code. Let's go!

4 Asynchronous Programming

Out of all chapters in this book, this is my favorite, because I've faced the consequences of bad asynchronous programming in the past, with callbacks on event listeners, HTTP requests, and basically everything that requires latency.

JavaScript has evolved from all these cluttered, unreadable, unmaintainable programming practices and that's what we're going to learn in this chapter.

Anyway, let's learn what an asynchronous program is. You can think of an asynchronous program as a program consisting of two lines of code, say L1 and L2. Now, we all know that in a given file, the code always executes from top to bottom. Also, it is intuitive such that the code will wait for each line to complete before executing the next line.

In the case of asynchronous programming, the code will execute L1, but it will not block L2 till L1 is completed. You can think of it as a kind of *non-blocking* programming.

In this chapter, we'll cover:

- The JavaScript execution model
- Event loops
- The difficulties faced while writing asynchronous code
- What are promises?
- Creating and working with promises
- How async/await differs from promises
- Advanced asynchronous programming with async/await

Let's start!

JavaScript execution model

JavaScript code is executed in a single thread, that is, two pieces of a script cannot run at the same time. Each website opened in the browser gets a single thread for downloading, parsing, and executing the website, called the main thread.

The main thread also maintains a queue, which has asynchronous tasks queued to be executed one by one. These queued tasks can be event handlers, callbacks, or any other kind of task. New tasks are added to the queue as AJAX requests/responses happen, events occur, timers are registered, and more. One long-running queue task can stop the execution of all other queue tasks and the main script. The main thread executes the tasks in this queue whenever possible.

HTML5 introduced web workers, which are actual threads running parallel to the main thread. When a web worker finishes executing or needs to notify the main thread, it simply adds a new event item to the queue. We'll discuss web workers separately in `Chapter 9`, *JavaScript on the Web*.

The event loop

JavaScript follows an *event loop-based* model in how it works. This is very different from languages such as Java. Although modern JavaScript compilers implement a very complex and heavily optimized version of the event loop model, we can still basically understand how the event loop works.

The call stack

JavaScript is a single-threaded language. That means it can have one call stack at a given time (take one thread = one call stack). Furthermore, it implies that JavaScript cannot do more than two things at a time. Or can it?

When you call a function, you step inside that function. This function is added to the call stack. When the function returns a value, the function is popped from the call stack.

Let's take a look at this example:

```
const page1 = $.syncHTTP('http://example.com/page1');
const page2 = $.syncHTTP('http://example.com/page2');
const page3 = $.syncHTTP('http://example.com/page3');
const page4 = $.syncHTTP('http://example.com/page4');

console.log(page1, page2, page3, page4);
```

For the sake of simplicity, consider `$.syncHTTP` as a predefined method that performs **synchronous** HTTP requests, that is, it'll block the code until completed. Let's assume every request takes ~500 ms to complete. Thus, if all these requests fire on clicking, say, a button, JavaScript immediately blocks the browser from doing anything for two seconds! That kills the user experience by a factor of 100!

Clearly, the call stack will consist of the first request, then after 500ms it'll remove that from the call stack, go to the second request, add that to the call stack, wait for 500ms for the response to receive, remove that from the call stack, and so on.

However, something strange happens when we make use of an asynchronous function such as `setTimeout()`. Take a look at this example:

```
console.log('Start');

setTimeout( () => {
  console.log('Middle');
}, 1000 )

console.log('End');
```

Here, as you expect, we'll first get `Start` printed because the call stack adds `console.log` to the stack, executes it, and removes it from the stack. Then the JavaScript comes to `setTimeout()`, adds it to the call stack, magically removes it without doing anything (more on this later), comes to the final `console.log`, adds it to the call stack, executes it to show `End`, and removes it from the stack.

Finally, magically, after 1 second, another `console.log` appears on the call stack, gets executed to print `Middle`, and then gets removed from the call stack.

Let's understand this magic.

Stack, queue, and Web APIs

So what happened when we called `setTimeout()` in the previous code? Where did it magically disappear from the call stack, making room for the next function execution?

Well, `setTimeout()` is a web API provided by each browser individually. When you call setTimeout, the call stack sends the `setTimeout()` function call to the Web API, which then keeps track of the timer (in our case) till it's complete.

Once the Web API realizes the timer is complete, it does not immediately push the contents back to the stack. It pushes a callback of the `setTimeout()` function to something known as a queue. A Queue, as the name implies, could be a queue of functions to be executed.

This is when the event loop comes into play. The event loop is a simple little tool that looks at the stack and queue all the time and sees if the stack is empty; if the queue has something it takes it from the queue and pushes it to the stack.

So essentially, once you're out of the call stack (async function), your function has to wait for the call stack to get emptied before it gets executed.

Based upon the previous line, guess the output of this code:

```
console.log('Hello');
setTimeout( () => {
  console.log('World')
}, 0 ) // 0 second timeout (executes immediately)
console.log('???')
```

Take a moment to think about this. When you're ready, see the answer as follows:

```
Hello
???
World
```

Now the reason for this is, when you call `setTimeout()`, it is cleared off from the call stack and the next function is called. The Web API finds that the timer for `setTimeout()` is over and pushes it to a queue. The event loop waits for the final `console.log` statement to finish before pushing the callback function of `setTimeout()` to the stack. And thus we get the output shown earlier.

The following figure illustrates the previous code:

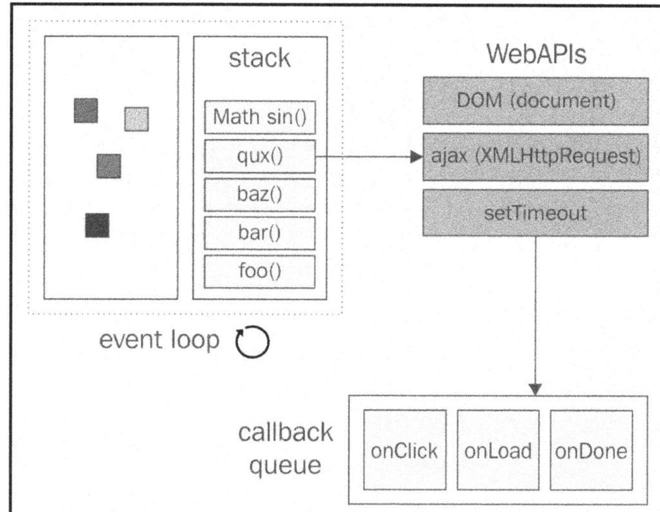

Writing asynchronous code

Although modern JavaScript brings promises and ES8 brings in async/await (which we'll see soon), still, there will be times when you'll encounter old APIs using callback mechanism/event-based mechanisms for their asynchronous operations.

It is important to understand the working of older asynchronous coding practices. This is because you cannot convert a callback-based asynchronous code piece to shining promises/async-await-based code without actually understanding how it works!

JavaScript, earlier, natively supported two patterns for writing asynchronous code, that is, the event pattern and the callback pattern. While writing asynchronous code, we usually start an asynchronous operation and register the event handlers or pass the callbacks, which will be executed once the operation is finished.

Event handlers or callbacks are used, depending on how the specific asynchronous API is designed. An API that is designed for an event pattern can be wrapped with some custom code to create the callback pattern for the API, and vice-versa. For example, AJAX is designed for the event pattern, but jQuery AJAX exposes it as a callback pattern. Let's consider some examples of writing asynchronous code involving events and callbacks and their difficulties.

Asynchronous code involving events

For asynchronous JavaScript APIs involving events, you need to register the success and error event handlers that will be executed depending on whether the operation was a success or failure respectively.

For example, while making an AJAX request, we register the event handlers that will be executed depending on whether the AJAX request was made successfully or not. Consider this code snippet, which makes an AJAX request and logs the retrieved information:

```
function displayName(json) {
    try {
        //we usally display it using DOM
        console.log(json.Name);
    } catch(e) {
    console.log("Exception: " + e.message);
    }
}

function displayProfession(json) {
    try {
        console.log(json.Profession);
    } catch(e) {
        console.log("Exception: " + e.message);
    }
}

function displayAge(json) {
    try {
        console.log(json.Age);
    } catch(e) {
        console.log("Exception: " + e.message);
    }
}

function displayData(data) {
    try {
        const json = JSON.parse(data);
        displayName(json);
        displayProfession(json);
        displayAge(json);
    } catch(e) {
        console.log("Exception: " + e.message);
    }
}

const request = new XMLHttpRequest();
```

```
const url = "data.json";
request.open("GET", url);
request.addEventListener("load", function(){

    if(request.status === 200) {
        displayData(request.responseText);
    } else {
        console.log("Server Error: " + request.status);
    }

}, false);

request.addEventListener("error", function(){
    console.log("Cannot Make AJAX Request");
}, false);

request.send();
```

Here, we assume the `data.json` file to have this content:

```
{
    "Name": "Eden",
    "Profession": "Developer",
    "Age": "25"
}
```

The `send()` method of the `XMLHttpRequest()` object is executed asynchronously, and retrieves the `data.json` file and calls the load or error event handler depending on whether the request was made successfully or not.

There is absolutely no issue with how this AJAX works, but the issue is how we write the code involving events. Here are the issues that we faced while writing the previous code:

- We had to add an exception handler for every block of code that will be executed asynchronously. We can't just wrap the whole code using a single `try` and `catch` statement. This makes it difficult to catch the exceptions.
- The code is harder to read, as it's difficult to follow the code flow due to the nested function calls.

If another part of the program wants to know if the asynchronous operation is finished, pending, or being executed then we have to maintain custom variables for that purpose. So we can say it is difficult to find the state of an asynchronous operation. This code can get even more complicated and harder to read if you are nesting multiple AJAX or any other asynchronous operations. For example, after displaying the data, you may want to ask the user to verify if the data is correct or not, and then send the Boolean value back to the server. Here is the code example to demonstrate this:

```
function verify() {
    try {
        const result = confirm("Is the data correct?");
        if (result) {
        //make AJAX request to send data to server
        } else {
        //make AJAX request to send data to server
        }
    } catch(e) {
        console.log("Exception: " + e.message);
    }
}

function displayData(data) {
    try {
        const json = JSON.parse(data);
        displayName(json);
        displayProfession(json);
        displayAge(json);
        verify();
    } catch(e) {
        console.log("Exception: " + e.message);
    }
}
```

Asynchronous code involving callbacks

For asynchronous JavaScript APIs involving callbacks, you need to pass success and error callbacks, which will be called depending on whether the operation was a success or failure respectively. For example, while making an AJAX request using jQuery, we need to pass the callbacks, which will be executed depending on whether the AJAX request was made successfully or not. Consider this code snippet that makes an AJAX request using jQuery and logs the retrieved information:

```
function displayName(json) {
    try {
```

```
        console.log(json.Name);
    } catch(e) {
        console.log("Exception: " + e.message);
    }
}

function displayProfession(json) {
    try {
        console.log(json.Profession);
    } catch(e) {
        console.log("Exception: " + e.message);
    }
}

function displayAge(json) {
    try {
        console.log(json.Age);
    } catch(e) {
        console.log("Exception: " + e.message);
    }
}

function displayData(data) {
    try {
        const json = JSON.parse(data);
        displayName(json);
        displayProfession(json);
        displayAge(json);
    } catch(e) {
        console.log("Exception: " + e.message);
    }
}

$.ajax({
url: "data.json",
success: function(result, status, responseObject) {
    displayData(responseObject.responseText);
},
error: function(xhr,status,error) {
    console.log("Cannot Make AJAX Request. Error is: " + error);
}
});
```

Even here, there is absolutely no issue with how this jQuery AJAX works, but the issue is how we write the code involving callbacks. Here are the issues that we faced while writing the preceding code:

- It is difficult to catch the exceptions, as we have to use multiple `try` and `catch` statements.
- The code is harder to read, as it's difficult to follow the code flow due to the nested function calls.
- It's difficult to maintain the state of the asynchronous operation. This code will get even more complicated if we nest multiple jQuery AJAX or any other asynchronous operations.

Promises and async programming

JavaScript now has a new native pattern for writing asynchronous code called the **Promise** pattern. This new pattern removes the common code issues that the event and callback pattern had. It also makes the code look more like synchronous code. A promise (or a `Promise` object) represents an asynchronous operation. Existing asynchronous JavaScript APIs are usually wrapped with promises, and the new JavaScript APIs are purely implemented using promises. Promises are new in JavaScript but are already present in many other programming languages. Programming languages, such as C# 5, C++ 11, Swift, Scala, and more are some examples that support promises.
Let's see how to use promises.

Promise states

A promise is always in one of these states:

- **Fulfilled:** If the resolve callback is invoked with a non-promise object as the argument or no argument, then we say that the promise is fulfilled
- **Rejected:** If the rejecting callback is invoked or an exception occurs in the executor scope, then we say that the promise is rejected
- **Pending:** If the resolve or reject callback is yet to be invoked, then we say that the promise is pending
- **Settled:** A promise is said to be settled if it's either fulfilled or rejected, but not pending

Once a promise is fulfilled or rejected, it cannot be transitioned back. An attempt to transition it will have no effect.

Promises versus callbacks

Suppose you wanted to perform three AJAX requests one after another. Here's a dummy implementation of that in callback-style:

```
ajaxCall('http://example.com/page1', response1 => {
   ajaxCall('http://example.com/page2'+response1, response2 => {
     ajaxCall('http://example.com/page3'+response2, response3 => {
       console.log(response3)
     }
   })
})
```

You can see how quickly you can enter into something known as **callback-hell**. Multiple nesting makes code not only unreadable but also difficult to maintain. Furthermore, if you start processing data after every call, and the next call is based on a previous call's response data, the complexity of the code will be unmatchable.

Callback-hell refers to multiple asynchronous functions nested inside each other's callback functions. This makes code harder to read and maintain.

Promises can be used to flatten this code. Let's take a look:

```
ajaxCallPromise('http://example.com/page1')
.then( response1 => ajaxCallPromise('http://example.com/page2'+response1) )
.then( response2 => ajaxCallPromise('http://example.com/page3'+response2) )
.then( response3 => console.log(response3) )
```

You can see the code complexity is suddenly reduced and the code looks much cleaner and readable. Let's first see how `ajaxCallPromise` would've been implemented.

Please read the following explanation for more clarity of preceding code snippet.

Promise constructor and (resolve, reject) methods

To convert an existing *callback type* function to `Promise`, we have to use the `Promise` constructor. In the preceding example, `ajaxCallPromise` returns a `Promise`, which can be either **resolved** or **rejected** by the developer. Let's see how to implement `ajaxCallPromise`:

```
const ajaxCallPromise = url => {
  return new Promise((resolve, reject) => {
    // DO YOUR ASYNC STUFF HERE
    $.ajaxAsyncWithNativeAPI(url, function(data) {
      if(data.resCode === 200) {
          resolve(data.message)
      } else {
          reject(data.error)
      }
    })
  })
}
```

Hang on! What just happened there?

1. First, we returned `Promise` from the `ajaxCallPromise` function. That means whatever we do now will be a `Promise`.
2. A `Promise` accepts a function argument, with the function itself accepting two very special arguments, that is, resolve and reject.
3. `resolve` and `reject` are themselves functions.
4. When, inside a `Promise` constructor function body, you call `resolve` or `reject`, the promise acquires a *resolved* or *rejected* value that is unchangeable later on.
5. We then make use of the native callback-based API and check if everything is OK. If everything is indeed OK, we resolve the `Promise` with the value being the message sent by the server (assuming a JSON response).
6. If there was an error in the response, we reject the promise instead.

You can return a promise in a then call. When you do that, you can flatten the code instead of chaining promises again.

For example, if `foo()` and `bar()` both return `Promise`, `then`, instead of:

```
foo().then( res => {
   bar().then( res2 => {
     console.log('Both done')
   })
})
```

We can write it as follows:

```
foo()
.then( res => bar() ) // bar() returns a Promise
.then( res => {
   console.log('Both done')
})
```

This flattens the code.

The then(onFulfilled, onRejected) method

The `then()` method of a `Promise` object lets us do a task after a `Promise` has been fulfilled or rejected. The task can also be another event-driven or callback-based asynchronous operation.

The `then()` method of a `Promise` object takes two arguments, that is, the `onFulfilled` and `onRejected` callbacks. The `onFulfilled` callback is executed if the `Promise` object was fulfilled, and the `onRejected` callback is executed if the `Promise` was rejected.

The `onRejected` callback is also executed if an exception is thrown in the scope of the executor. Therefore, it behaves like an exception handler, that is, it catches the exceptions. The `onFulfilled` callback takes a parameter, that is, the fulfilment value of the promise. Similarly, the `onRejected` callback takes a parameter, that is, the reason for rejection:

```
ajaxCallPromise('http://example.com/page1').then(
  successData => { console.log('Request was successful') },
  failData => { console.log('Request failed' + failData) }
)
```

When we reject the promise inside the `ajaxCallPromise` definition, the second function will execute (`failData` one) instead of the first function.

Let's take one more example by converting `setTimeout()` from a callback to a promise. This is how `setTimeout()` looks:

```
setTimeout( () => {
  // code here executes after TIME_DURATION milliseconds
}, TIME_DURATION)
```

A promised version will look something like the following:

```
const PsetTimeout = duration => {
   return new Promise((resolve, reject) => {
      setTimeout( () => {
         resolve()
      }, duration);
   })
}

// usage:

PsetTimeout(1000)
.then(() => {
  console.log('Executes after a second')
})
```

Here we resolved the promise without a value. If you do that, it gets resolved with a value equal to undefined.

The catch(onRejected) method

The `catch()` method of a `Promise` object is used instead of the `then()` method when we use the `then()` method only to handle errors and exceptions. There is nothing special about how the `catch()` method works. It's just that it makes the code much easier to read, as the word *catch* makes it more meaningful.

The `catch()` method just takes one argument, that is, the `onRejected` callback. The `onRejected` callback of the `catch()` method is invoked in the same way as the `onRejected` callback of the `then()` method.
The `catch()` method always returns a promise. Here is how a new `Promise` object is returned by the `catch()` method:

- If there is no return statement in the `onRejected` callback, then a new fulfilled `Promise` is created internally and returned.

- If we return a custom `Promise`, then it internally creates and returns a new `Promise` object. The new promise object resolves the custom promise object.
- If we return something else other than a custom `Promise` in the `onRejected` callback, then a new `Promise` object is created internally and returned. The new `Promise` object resolves the returned value.
- If we pass null instead of the `onRejected` callback or omit it, then a callback is created internally and used instead. The internally created `onRejected` callback returns a rejected `Promise` object. The reason for the rejection of the new `Promise` object is the same as the reason for the rejection of a parent `Promise` object.
- If the `Promise` object to which `catch()` is called gets fulfilled, then the `catch()` method simply returns a new fulfilled promise object and ignores the `onRejected` callback. The fulfillment value of the new `Promise` object is the same as the fulfillment value of the parent `Promise`.

To understand the `catch()` method, consider this code:

```
ajaxPromiseCall('http://invalidURL.com')
.then(success => { console.log(success) },
failed => { console.log(failed) });
```

This code can be rewritten in this way using the `catch()` method:

```
ajaxPromiseCall('http://invalidURL.com')
.then(success => console.log(success))
.catch(failed => console.log(failed));
```

These two code snippets work more or less in the same way.

The Promise.resolve(value) method

The `resolve()` method of the `Promise` object takes a value and returns a `Promise` object that resolves the passed value. The `resolve()` method is basically used to convert a value to a `Promise` object. It is useful when you find yourself with a value that may or may not be a `Promise`, but you want to use it as a `Promise`. For example, jQuery promises have different interfaces from ES6 promises. Therefore, you can use the `resolve()` method to convert jQuery promises into ES6 promises.

Here is an example that demonstrates how to use the `resolve()` method:

```
const p1 = Promise.resolve(4);
p1.then(function(value){
  console.log(value);
}); //passed a promise object

Promise.resolve(p1).then(function(value){
 console.log(value);
});

Promise.resolve({name: "Eden"})
.then(function(value){
  console.log(value.name);
});
```

The output is as follows:

```
4
4
Eden
```

The Promise.reject(value) method

The `reject()` method of the `Promise` object takes a value and returns a rejected `Promise` object with the passed value as the reason. Unlike the `Promise.resolve()` method, the `reject()` method is used for debugging purposes and not for converting values into promises.

Here is an example that demonstrates how to use the `reject()` method:

```
const p1 = Promise.reject(4);
p1.then(null, function(value){
console.log(value);
});
Promise.reject({name: "Eden"})
.then(null, function(value){
console.log(value.name);
});
```

The output is as follows:

```
4
Eden
```

The Promise.all(iterable) method

The `all()` method of the `Promise` object takes an iterable object as an argument and returns a `Promise` that fulfills when all of the promises in the iterable object have been fulfilled.

This can be useful when we want to execute a task after some asynchronous operations have finished. Here is a code example that demonstrates how to use the `Promise.all()` method:

```
const p1 = new Promise(function(resolve, reject){
 setTimeout(function(){
  resolve();
 }, 1000);
});

const p2 = new Promise(function(resolve, reject){
 setTimeout(function(){
  resolve();
 }, 2000);
});

const arr = [p1, p2];
Promise.all(arr).then(function(){
console.log("Done"); //"Done" is logged after 2 seconds
});
```

If the iterable object contains a value that is not a `Promise` object, then it's converted to the `Promise` object using the `Promise.resolve()` method.

If any of the passed promises get rejected, then the `Promise.all()` method immediately returns a new rejected `Promise` for the same reason as the rejected passed `Promise`. Here is an example to demonstrate this:

```
const p1 = new Promise(function(resolve, reject){
 setTimeout(function(){
  reject("Error");
 }, 1000);
});

const p2 = new Promise(function(resolve, reject){
 setTimeout(function(){
  resolve();
 }, 2000);
});
```

```
const arr = [p1, p2];
Promise.all(arr).then(null, function(reason){
console.log(reason); //"Error" is logged after 1 second
});
```

The Promise.race(iterable) method

The `race()` method of the `Promise` object takes an iterable object as the argument and returns a `Promise` that fulfills or rejects as soon as one of the promises in the iterable object is fulfilled or rejected, with the fulfillment value or reason from that `Promise`.

As the name suggests, the `race()` method is used to race between promises and see which one finishes first. Here is a code example that shows how to use the `race()` method:

```
var p1 = new Promise(function(resolve, reject){
setTimeout(function(){
resolve("Fulfillment Value 1");
}, 1000);
});
var p2 = new Promise(function(resolve, reject){
setTimeout(function(){
resolve("fulfillment Value 2");
}, 2000);
});
var arr = [p1, p2];
Promise.race(arr).then(function(value){
console.log(value); //Output "Fulfillment value 1"
}, function(reason){
console.log(reason);
});
```

Now at this point, I assume you have a basic understanding of how promises work, what they are, and how to convert a callback-like API into a promised API. Let's take a look at **async/await**, the future of asynchronous programming.

async/await – the future of asynchronous programming

To be honest, async/await blows away whatever you read previously about promises. But hey! You obviously need to know how promises work in order to know how to work with async/await. async/await are built on top of promises; however, once you get used to them, there is no going back to promises (unless, again, you need to convert a callback type API to async/await (you need to use promises for that).)

About async/await:

- It's for asynchronous coding
- It makes code look extremely similar to synchronous coding and thus makes it extremely powerful and easy on the eyes
- It is built on top of promises
- It makes error handling a cake walk. You can finally use `try` and `catch` with asynchronous coding!
- ES8 introduced async/await and, by the time you're reading this, it will have been implemented in all browsers natively (at the time of writing, only IE and Opera don't support async/await)

async/await versus promises

Although async/await are actually promises under the hood, they help a lot by adding a ton of readability to code. On the surface level, I believe a developer should be aware of minute differences in the usage of async/await versus promises. Here's a glimpse of these:

async/await	**promises**
Extremely clean code base	Uglier codebase with nested promises
Error handling with native `try-catch` blocks	Separate `catch()` method for error handling
Syntactic sugar for promises (built on promises)	Native implementation in standard
Introduced in ES8	Introduced in ES6

The async function and await keyword

In order to use the `await` keyword, we need to have an `async` function. The difference between a function and an `async` function is that the `async` function is followed by an *async* keyword. Let's take a look at an example:

```
async function ES8isCool() {
   // asynchronous work
   const information = await getES8Information() // Here getES8Information
itself is an async function
}
```

This is the crux of the thing. You can only use `await` inside an `async` function. This is because, when you call an `async` function, it returns a `Promise`. However, instead of using then with it, which eventually makes it a promise chain, we use the `await` keyword in front of it to kind of pause the execution *(not really)* inside the `async` function context.

Let's take a look at a real example:

```
function sendAsyncHTTP(url) {
 return new Promise((resolve, reject) => {
  const xhttp = new XMLHttpRequest()
  xhttp.onreadystatechange = function() {
    if (this.readyState == 4) { // success
    if(this.status == 200) {
           resolve(xhttp.responseText)
      } else {
           console.log(this.readyState, this.status)
           reject(xhttp.statusText) // failed
      }
    }
  };
  xhttp.open("GET", url, true);
  xhttp.send();
 })
}

async function doSomeTasks() {
   const documentFile1 = await sendAsyncHTTP('http://example.com')
   console.log('Got first document')
   const documentFile2 = await
sendAsyncHTTP('http://example.com/?somevar=true')
   console.log('Got second document')
   return documentFile2
}
```

```
doSomeTasks() // returns a Promise
.then( res => console.log("res is a HTML file") )
```

OK! First things first. Remember that an async function returns a `Promise`? Why didn't we use the `async` keyword with `sendAsyncHTTP`? Why did we return a `Promise` from `sendAsyncHTTP`? Why won't the code below work?

```
async function sendAsyncHTTP(url) {
  const xhttp = new XMLHttpRequest()
  xhttp.onreadystatechange = function() { // <-- hint
    if(this.status == 200) {
          resolve(xhttp.responseText)
     } else {
          console.log(this.readyState, this.status)
          reject(xhttp.statusText) // failed
     }
  };
  xhttp.open("GET", url, true);
  xhttp.send();
}
```

Carefully take a look at the hint comment line. Since we're using a function in `onreadystatechange`, returning inside that function does not return the parent function. So essentially, you return `undefined` from the `sendAsyncHTTP` function instead of a valid response. Had there been other async functions used with the `await` keyword, we could've returned a value without making use of the `new Promise()` declaration.

Confused? Stay with me. If you didn't really get what happened previously, continue reading. You will. Take a look at the next function:

```
async function doSomeTasks() {
   const documentFile1 = await sendAsyncHTTP('http://example.com')
   console.log('Got first document')
   const documentFile2 = await
sendAsyncHTTP('http://example.com/?somevar=true')
   console.log('Got second document')
   return documentFile2
}
```

Look carefully! We didn't return a `Promise` here by using `return new Promise`. Why does this work then? This is because this function actually waits for an `async` function using the `await` keyword. See, when the code comes to `Line 1`, it halts before executing the next line `(console.log('Got first document'))`.

Whenever JavaScript finds await followed by a function that returns a `Promise`, it will wait for that promise to either resolve or reject. In our case, `sendAsyncHTTP` resolves with the source code of the website, so we get that back in the `documentFile2` variable.

We do a similar thing again but with a slightly different URL this time. And once we're done with both, we return `documentFile2`. Hang on here. Remember again, the `async function` returns a `Promise`. That means, whatever value you return from an `async` function, it is actually the resolved value of that returned `Promise`. And whatever value you `throw` inside the `async` function, it goes as the rejected value of that returned `Promise`. This is important!

Finally, we called `doSomeTasks()`, and as mentioned it returned a `Promise`. Therefore, you can use a then chain with it to just log to the console that everything was done. The `res` variable consists of whatever value you returned. The `catch()` method will catch any error you throw inside the `async` function.

Making asynchronous code look synchronous

Try to convert the following `Promise` code to async/await:

```
const doSomething = () => {
  return p1().then(res1 => {
      return p2().then(res2 => {
          // finally we need both res1 and res2
          return p3(res1, res2)
        })
    })
}
```

You see? Even with promises, you cannot avoid nesting if you need to make use of the first promise's value somewhere down the chain. This is because, if you flatten out the promise chain, you eventually lose the previous promise's returned values.

Ready for the answer? Here you go:

```
const doSomething = async () => {
  const res1 = await p1()
  const res2 = await p2()
  return p3(res1, res2)
}
```

Can you see the code clarity in the latter code? It is remarkable! Try to use async/await wherever you can, instead of callbacks or promises.

Summary

In this chapter, we learned how JavaScript executes asynchronous code. We learned about event loops, and basically how JavaScript manages all asynchronous and multiple tasks without using any additional threads. We learned about different patterns for writing asynchronous code.

We saw how promises make it easier to read and write asynchronous code, and how async/await blows away promises in practice. In the next chapter, we'll take a look at how to organize your JavaScript code with a modular programming approach.

5
Modular Programming

Modular programming is one of the most important and frequently used software design techniques. Modular programming basically means splitting your code into multiple files that are usually independent of each other. This makes it a cake-walk when managing and maintaining different modules of a program. It helps in debugging nasty bugs easily, pushing updates to a particular module, and so on.

Unfortunately, for a long time, JavaScript didn't support modules natively; that led programmers to use alternative techniques to achieve modular programming in JavaScript. However, ES6 introduced a native modular technique in JavaScript for the first time.

This chapter is all about how to create and import JavaScript modules. In this chapter, we will first learn how modules were created earlier, and then we will jump to the new built-in JavaScript module system.

In this chapter, we'll cover:

- What is modular programming?
- The benefits of modular programming
- The basics of IIFE modules, AMD, UMD, and CommonJS
- Creating and importing ES6 modules
- Implementing modules in browsers

JavaScript modules 101

The practice of breaking down programs and libraries into modules is called modular programming.

In JavaScript, a **module** is a collection of related objects, functions, and other components of a program or library that are wrapped together and isolated from the scope of the rest of the program or library.

A module exports some variables to the outside program to let it access the components wrapped by the module. To use a module, a program needs to import the module and the variables exported by the module.

A module can also be split into further modules called sub-modules, thus creating a module hierarchy.

Modular programming has many benefits. Some benefits are as follows:

- It keeps our code both cleanly separated and organized by splitting it into multiple modules
- Modular programming leads to fewer global variables, that is, it eliminates the problem of global variables, because modules don't interface via the global scope, and each module has its own scope
- It makes code reusability easier as importing and using the same modules in different projects is easier
- It allows many programmers to collaborate on the same program or library, by making each programmer work on a particular module with a particular functionality
- Bugs in an application can easily be easily identified as they are localized to a particular module

Implementing modules – the old way

Before ES6, JavaScript had never supported modules natively. Developers used other techniques and third-party libraries to implement modules in JavaScript. Using **Immediately-Invoked Function Expression** (**IIFE**), **Asynchronous Module Definition** (**AMD**), CommonJS, and **Universal Module Definition** (**UMD**) are various popular ways of implementing modules in ES5. As these ways were not native to JavaScript, they had several problems. Let's take an overview of each of these old ways of implementing modules.

Immediately-Invoked Function Expression (IIFE)

We've briefly discussed IIFE functions in earlier chapters. It is basically an anonymous function that is executed automatically. Let's take a look at one example. This is how a typical old JS module that uses IIFE looks:

```
//Module Starts

(function(window){
const sum =(x, y) => x + y;
const sub = (x,y) => x - y;
const math = {
  findSum(a, b) { return sum(a, b) },
  findSub(a,b) { return sub(a, b) }
}
window.math = math;
})(window)

//Module Ends

console.log(math.findSum(1, 2)); //Output "3"
console.log(math.findSub(1, 2)); //Output "-1"
```

Here, we created a module using IIFE. The `sum` and `sub` variables are global to the module, but not visible outside the module. The `math` variable is exported by the module to the main program to expose the functionalities that it provides.

This module works completely independently of the program and can be imported by any other program by simply copying it into the source code, or importing it as a separate file (by including it as script src, or by using external libraries).

The reason it'll work is that ultimately you're attaching the `math` object to the window (which is global).

A library using IIFE, such as jQuery, wraps all of its APIs in a single IIFE module. When a program uses a jQuery library, it automatically imports the module.

Asynchronous Module Definition (AMD)

AMD is a specification for implementing modules in the browser. AMD is designed by keeping browser limitations in mind, that is, it imports modules asynchronously to prevent blocking the loading of a webpage. As AMD is not a native browser specification, we need to use an AMD library.

RequireJS is the most popular AMD library. Let's see an example of how to create and import modules using RequireJS. According to the AMD specification, every module needs to be represented by a separate file. So first, create a file named `math.js` that represents a module. Here is the sample code that will be inside the module:

```
define(function(){
  const sum = (x, y) => x + y
  const sub = (x, y) => x - y
  const math = {
    findSum(a, b) { return sum(a,b) },
    findSub(a, b){ return sub(a, b); }
  }
  return math;
});
```

Here, the module exports the `math` variable to expose its functionality.

Now, let's create a file named `index.js`, to act as the main program that imports the module and exported variables. Here is the code that will be inside the `index.js` file:

```
require(["math"], function(math){
  console.log(math.findSum(1, 2)); //Output "3"
  console.log(math.findSub(1, 2)); //Output "-1"
})
```

Here, the `math` variable in the first parameter is the name of the file that is treated as the AMD module. The `.js` extension added to the file name is added automatically by RequireJS.

The `math` variable, which is in the second parameter, references the exported variable. Here, the module is imported asynchronously, and the callback is also executed asynchronously.

You can learn more about RequireJS and its usage here: `http://bit.ly/requirejs-tutorials`.

CommonJS

CommonJS is the most widely used, unofficial spec right now. CommonJS is a specification for implementing modules in Node.js. According to the CommonJS specification, every module needs to be represented by a separate file. CommonJS modules are imported **synchronously**. This is the reason why browsers do not use CommonJS as a module loader!

Let's see an example of how to create and import modules using CommonJS. First, we will create a file named `math.js` that represents a module. Here is sample code that will be inside the module:

```
const sum =(x, y) => x + y;
const sub = (x, y) => x - y;
const math = {
  findSum(a, b) {
    return sum(a,b);
  },
  findSub(a, b){
    return sub(a, b);
  }
}

exports.math = math; // or module.exports.math = math
```

Here, the module exports the `math` variable to expose its functionality. Now, let's create a file named `index.js`, to act as the main program that imports the module.

Here is the code that will be inside the `index.js` file:

```
const math = require("./math").math;
console.log(math.findSum(1, 2)); //Output "3"
console.log(math.findSub(1, 2)); //Output "-1"
```

Here, the `math` variable is the name of the file that is treated as a module. The `.js` extension to the file name is added automatically by CommonJS.

exports versus module.exports

Previously, we said that you can use `exports.math` or `module.exports.math` in order to export a variable from the module. What's the difference between two?

Well, technically, exports and `module.exports` point to the same object. You can think about this in the following manner:

```
exports = module.exports = { }
```

This is how it starts. Now it doesn't matter whether you assign a property value to `module.exports` or exports because they both point to the same object. However, you must remember that it is `module.exports` that is actually exported!

For example, consider `string1.js`, `string2.js`, and `index.js`.

`string1.js` is shown as follows:

```
// string1.js
module.exports = () => "Amazing string" // correct export of function
```

`string2.js` is shown as follows:

```
// string2.js
exports = () => "Amazing string" // this fails to export this function
```

`index.js` is shown as follows:

```
// index.js
console.log(require('string1.js')()); // <-- we're executing the imported
function
console.log(require('string2.js')());
```

What do you think the output is?

Clearly, as we said previously, `exports` is not exported. Thus, the second call (`require('string2.js')()`) throws an error because `require('string2.js')` returns an empty object (thus you cannot execute it as a function).

On the other hand, when `module.exports` is changed from an object to a function, the function is exported and then invoked by the developer in the first line call `(string1.js)`.

Universal Module Definition (UMD)

We saw three different specifications for implementing modules. These three specifications have their own respective ways of creating and importing modules. Wouldn't it be great if we could create modules that were imported as an IIFE, AMD, or CommonJS module?

UMD is a set of techniques that are used to create modules that can be imported as an IIFE, CommonJS, or AMD module. Therefore, now a program can import third-party modules, irrespective of what module specification it is using.

The most popular UMD technique is `returnExports`. According to the `returnExports` technique, every module needs to be represented by a separate file. So, let's create a file named `math.js` that represents a module. Here is the sample code that will be inside the module:

```
(function (root, factory) {
  //Environment Detection
  if (typeof define === 'function' && define.amd) {
    define([], factory);
  } else if (typeof exports === 'object') {
    module.exports = factory();
  } else {
    root.returnExports = factory();
  }
}(this, function () {
//Module Definition
  const sum = (x, y) => x + y;
  const sub = (x, y) => x - y;
  const math = {
    findSum(a, b) {
        return sum(a,b);
    },
    findSub(a, b) {
        return sub(a, b);
    }
  }
return math;
})
);
```

Now, you can successfully import the `math.js` module any way that you wish, for instance, by using CommonJS, RequireJS, or IIFE.

Implementing modules – the new way

There is a new way to import and export modules in JavaScript, that is the official module system. Since it is supported natively by the language, it can be referred to as the standard JavaScript module system. You should consider using the official module system in practice because it's native and thus optimized for speed and performance.

Importing/exporting modules

Let's say you're coding a module file and now you're ready to import it into your main file. How will you export it using the official module system? Here's how:

```
// module.js

const takeSquareAndAdd2 = num => {
    return num*num + 2;
}

export { takeSquareAndAdd2 }; // #1
export const someVariable = 100; // #2
export function yourName(name) {
    return `Your name ${name} is a nice name`
}; // #3
export default "Holy moly this is interesting!" // #4
```

- `#1`: We've first coded a function and then, using the `export` keyword, made it available to other modules that import this particular module.
- `#2`: You can directly declare, initialize, and export variables/functions in a single line.
- `#3`: As `#2` says, you can directly export the functions as you create them.
- `#4`: The previous three are called named exports, whereas this is a default export. We'll soon see the difference between the two.

Let's see how to import this previous module in a separate file:

```
// index.js
import myString, { takeSquareAndAdd2 } from './module.js'
console.log(myString) // "Holy moly this is interesting"
console.log(takeSquareAndAdd2(2)) // 6
```

Wait. What happened here? Let's study.

Named versus default exports

Earlier, we saw that we used the export default: *Holy moly this is interesting*. What it does is, when we use `import <varname> from './module'`, it assigns `<varname>` the value of the default export. Therefore, see the following:

```
// index.js
import string from './module.js'
console.log(string)
```

This will console-log *Holy moly this is interesting.*

This is called a default export.

A named export, on the other hand, has a name associated with it (the variable's name or the function's name). You'll have to import a named-export variable using destructuring syntax. This is because you can think of the `export` keyword as exporting a default value *plus* an object that contains all other exports you're doing (named exports).

Therefore, see the following:

```
import { takeSquareAndAdd2 } from './module.js';
console.log(takeSquareAndAdd2(3))
```

This will output `11`.

You cannot use `var/let/const` when doing an export default; just do `export default <YOUR VALUE HERE>`. However, you **can** do `export default` followed by a function.

Naming named imports

You can also change the name of a named export in the module to which you're importing it. This is achieved by using the `as` keyword:

```
import { takeSquareAndAdd2 as myFunc } from './module.js';
console.log(myFunc(3))
```

This will still produce the output `11`. This is essential when you have long module names or names that might conflict with your base code/other imported modules.

Similarly, you can rename some named imports, and leave the rest as it is:

```
import { takeSquareAndAdd2 as myFunc, yourName } from './module.js';
console.log(myFunc(3)) // 11
console.log(yourName("Mehul")) // Your name Mehul is a nice name
```

Wildcard imports

What if you want to import all the exported entities in the whole module? Writing each entity's name yourself is cumbersome; also, if you do that, you'll pollute the global scope. Let's see how we can fix both of these issues.

Let's assume our `module.js` looks something like this:

```
// module.js
export const PI = 3.14
export const sqrt3 = 1.73
export function returnWhatYouSay(text) { return text; }
```

Let's import everything at once:

```
// index.js
import * as myModule from './module.js'
console.log(myModule.PI) // 3.14
console.log(myModule.returnWhatYouSay("This is cool!"))
```

The asterisk (`*`) will import everything that is exported under the scope of the `myModule` object. It makes accessing all exported variables/methods cleaner.

Let's quickly gather all the information about the import/export syntax in the following sections.

Additional information on export

We need to use the export statement in a module to export variables. The export statement comes in many different formats. Here are the formats:

- `export {variableName}` - This format exports a variable
- `export {variableName1, variableName2, variableName3}` - This format is used to export multiple variables
- `export {variableName as myVariableName}` - This format is used to export a variable with another name, that is, an alias
- `export {variableName1 as myVariableName1, variableName2 as myVariableName2}` - This format is used to export multiple variables with different names
- `export {variableName as default}` - This format uses default as the alias

- `export {variableName as default, variableName1 as myVariableName1, variableName2}` - This format is similar to the fourth format, but it also has the default alias
- `export default function(){}` - This format works similarly to the fifth format, but here you can place an expression instead of a variable name
- `export {variableName1, variableName2} from "myAnotherModule"` - This format is used to export the exported variables of a submodule
- `export * from "myAnotherModule"` - This format is used to export all the exported variables of a submodule

Here are some important things that you need to know about the export statement:

- An export statement can be used anywhere in a module. It's not compulsory to use it at the end of the module.
- There can be any number of export statements in a module.
- You cannot export variables on demand. For example, placing the export statement in the `if...else` condition throws an error. Therefore, we can say that the module structure needs to be static, that is, exports can be determined at compile time.
- You cannot export the same variable name or alias multiple times. But you can export a variable multiple times with a different alias.
- All the code inside a module is executed in strict mode by default.
- The values of the exported variables can be changed inside the module that exported them.

Additional information on import

To `import` a module, we need to use the `import` statement. The `import` statement comes in many different formats. Here are the formats:

```
import x from "module-relative-path";
import {x} from "module-relative-path";
import {x1 as x2} from "module-relative-path";
import {x1, x2} from "module-relative-path";
import {x1, x2 as x3} from "module-relative-path";
import x, {x1, x2} from "module-relative-path";
import "module-relative-path";
import * as x from "module-relative-path";
import x1, * as x2 from "module-relative-path";
```

An `import` statement consists of two parts: the variable names we want to `import` and the `relative` path of the module.

Here are the differences in these formats:

- `import x from "module-relative-path"` - In this format, the default alias is imported. `x` is the alias of the default alias.
- `import {x} from "module-relative-path"` - In this format, the `x` variable is imported.
- `import {x1 as x2} from "module-relative-path"` - This format is the same as the second format. It's just that `x2` is an alias of `x1`.
- `import {x1, x2} from "module-relative-path"` - In this format, we import the `x1` and `x2` variables.
- `import {x1, x2 as x3} from "module-relative-path"` - In this format, we import the `x1` and `x2` variables. The `x3` is an alias of the `x2` variable.
- `import x, {x1, x2} from "module-relative-path"` - In this format, we import the `x1` and `x2` variable, and the default alias. The `x` is an alias of the default alias.
- `import "module-relative-path"` - In this format, we just `import` the module. We do not `import` any of the variables exported by the module.
- `import * as x from "module-relative-path"` - In this format, we `import` all the variables and wrap them in an object called `x`. Even the default alias is imported.
- `import x1, * as x2 from "module-relative-path"` - The ninth format is the same as the eighth format. Here, we give another alias to the default alias.

Here are some important things that you need to know about the import statement:

- While importing a variable, if we import it with an alias, then to refer to that variable we have to use the alias and not the actual variable name; that is, the actual variable name will not be visible, only the alias will be visible.
- The import statement doesn't import a copy of the exported variables; rather, it makes the variables available in the scope of the program that imports it. Therefore, if you make a change to an exported variable inside the module, then the change is visible to the program that imports it.
- Imported variables are read-only, that is, you cannot reassign them to something else outside the scope of the module that exports them.

- A module can only be imported once in a single instance of a JavaScript engine. If we try to import it again, then the already imported instance of the module will be used. (In other words, modules are singletons in JavaScript.)
- We cannot import modules on demand. For example, placing the import statement in the `if...else` condition throws an error. Therefore, we can say that imports should be able to be determined at compile time.

Tree shaking

Tree shaking is basically a term used by module bundlers such as WebPack and Rollup to convey that the import-export module syntax can be used for dead-code elimination.

Essentially, the new module loader system enables these module bundlers to do something known as tree shaking, where they shake the tree to get rid of the dead leaves.

Your JavaScript is a tree. The modules you import represent the living leaves of your tree. The dead (unused) code is represented by the brown, dead leaves of the tree. To remove dead leaves, the bundler has to shake the tree and let them fall.

How tree shaking is performed

Tree shaking, used by a module bundler, eliminates unused code in the following manner:

1. Firstly, the bundler will combine all of the imported module files (like a good bundler). Here, exports that are not imported in any file are not exported at all.
2. After that, the bundler minifies the bundle and simultaneously removes dead code. Thus, variables/functions that are not exported or used inside their respective module files are not present in the compressed bundle file. This way, tree shaking is performed.

Using modules on the web

Modern browsers have very recently started to implement module loaders natively. To natively use a script that imports modules, you'll have to make its `type="module"`.

Here's a very basic working example in Chrome 63:

```
// index.html
<!doctype HTML>
<html>
    <head>
        <script src="index.js" type="module"></script>
    </head>
    <body>
        <div id="text"></div>
    </body>
</html>
```

This is how `index.js` (the main script file) will look:

```
// index.js
import { writeText2Div as write2Div } from './module.js';
write2Div('Hello world!')
```

This is the module that `index.js` imports (in the same directory):

```
// module.js
const writeText2Div = text => document.getElementByID('text').innerText =
text;
export { writeText2Div };
```

This, when tested, should show `Hello World` on the screen.

Summary

In this chapter, we saw what modular programming is and learned different modular programming specifications. We learned about the future of modular programming and how to use it in web browsers for real projects. With the evolution of ECMAScript, we expect to see a further boost in features and performance, which will ultimately benefit both the end user and the developers.

In the next chapter, we're going to take a look at something known as the **Reflect API**, a shining new collection of methods for interceptable JavaScript operations.

6
Implementing the Reflect API

The Reflect API is used for object reflection (that is, inspecting and manipulating the properties of objects). Although ES5 already had APIs for object reflection, these APIs were not well organized and, on failure, used to throw an exception. The Reflect API is well organized and makes it easier to read and write code, as it doesn't throw exceptions on failure. Instead, it returns the Boolean value, representing if the operation was true or false. Since developers are adapting to the Reflect API for object reflection, it's important to learn this API in depth. In this chapter, we'll cover:

- Calling a function with a given `this` value
- Invoking a constructor with the prototype property of another constructor
- Defining or modifying the attributes of the object properties
- Enumerating the properties of an object using an iterator object
- Retrieving and setting the internal [[prototype]] property of an object
- A lot of other operations related to inspecting and manipulating methods and properties of objects

The Reflect object

The global `Reflect` object exposes all the new methods for object reflection. `Reflect` is not a function object; therefore, you cannot invoke the `Reflect` object. Also, you cannot use it with the `new` operator. All the methods of the Reflect API are wrapped in the `Reflect` object to make it look well organized.

The `Reflect` object provides many methods, which overlap with the global object's methods in terms of functionality. Let's see the various methods provided by the `Reflect` object for object reflection.

The Reflect.apply(function, this, args) method

The `Reflect.apply()` method is used to invoke a function with a given `this` value. The function invoked by `Reflect.apply()` is called as the target function. It's the same as the `apply()` method of the function object. The `Reflect.apply()` method takes three arguments:

- The first argument represents the target function.
- The second argument represents the value of `this` inside the target function. This argument is optional.
- The third argument is an array object, specifying the arguments of the target function. This argument is optional.

The `Reflect.apply()` method returns whatever the target function returns. Here is a code example to demonstrate how to use the `Reflect.apply()` method:

```
function function_name(a, b, c) {
  return this.value + a + b + c;
}
var returned_value = Reflect.apply(function_name, {value: 100}, [10, 20,
30]);
console.log(returned_value); //Output "160"
```

The Reflect.construct(constructor, args, prototype) method

The `Reflect.construct()` method is used to invoke a function as a constructor. It's similar to the `new` operator. The function that will be invoked is called as the target constructor.

One special reason why you may want to use the `Reflect.construct()` method instead of the `new` operator is that you can target the constructor's prototype to match the prototype of another constructor.

The `Reflect.construct()` method takes three arguments:

- The first argument is the target constructor.
- The second argument is an array, specifying the arguments of the target constructor. This argument is optional.
- The third argument is another constructor whose prototype will be used as the prototype of the target constructor. This argument is optional. The `Reflect.construct()` method returns the new instance created by the target constructor.

Here is the code example, to demonstrate how to use the `Reflect.constructor()` method:

```
function constructor1(a, b) {
  this.a = a;
  this.b = b;
  this.f = function(){
    return this.a + this.b + this.c;
  }
}
function constructor2(){
}
constructor2.prototype.c = 100;
var myObject = Reflect.construct(constructor1, [1,2], constructor2);
console.log(myObject.f()); //Output "103"
```

In the preceding example, we used the prototype chain of `consturctor2` as the prototype of `constructor1` while invoking `constructor1`.

The Reflect.defineProperty(object, property, descriptor) method

The `Reflect.defineProperty()` method defines a new property directly on an object or modifies an existing property on an object. It returns a Boolean value indicating whether the operation was successful or not.

It's similar to the `Object.defineProperty()` method. The difference is that the `Reflect.defineProperty()` method returns a Boolean, whereas the `Object.defineProperty()` returns the modified object. If the `Object.defineProperty()` method fails to modify or define an object property, then it throws an exception, whereas the `Reflect.defineProperty()` method returns a `false` result. The `Reflect.defineProperty()` method takes in three arguments:

- The first argument is the object that is used to define or modify a property
- The second argument is the symbol or name of the property that is to be defined or modified
- The third argument is the descriptor for the property that is being defined or modified

Understanding the data properties and accessor properties

Since ES5, every object property is either a data property or an accessor property. A data property has a value, which may or may not be writable, whereas an accessor property has a getter-setter pair of functions to set and retrieve the property value.

The attributes of a data property are `value`, `writable`, `enumerable`, and `configurable`. On the other hand, the attributes of an accessor property are `set`, `get`, `enumerable`, and `configurable`.

A descriptor is an object that describes the attributes of a property. When creating a property using the `Reflect.defineProperty()` method, the `Object.defineProperty()` method, the `Object.defineProperties()` method, or the `Object.create()` method, we need to pass a descriptor for the property.

A data property's descriptor object has the following properties:

- **Value:** This is the value associated with the property. The default value is `undefined`.
- **Writable:** If this is `true`, then the property value can be changed with an assignment operator. The default value is `false`.

- **Configurable:** If this is `true`, then the property attributes can be changed, and the property may be deleted. The default value is `false`. Remember, when the configurable attribute is `false` and the writable is `true`, the value and the writable attributes can be changed.
- **Enumerable:** If this is `true`, then the property shows up in the `for...in` loop and the `Object.keys()` method. The default value is `false`.

An accessor property's descriptor has the following properties:

- **Get:** This is a function that returns the property value. The function has no parameters and the default value is `undefined`.
- **Set:** This is a function that sets the property value. The function will receive the new value that is being assigned to the property.
- **Configurable:** If this is `true`, then the property descriptor can be changed and the property may be deleted. The default value is `false`.
- **Enumerable:** If this is `true`, then the property shows up in the `for...in` loop and the `Object.keys()` method. The default value is `false`.

Depending on the properties of the descriptor object, JavaScript decides whether the property is a data property or an accessor property.

If you add a property without using the `Reflect.defineProperty()` method, the `Object.defineProperty()` method, the `Object.defineProperties()` method, or the `Object.create()` method, then the property is a data property and the writable, enumerable, and configurable attributes are all set to `true`. After the property is added, you can modify its attributes.

If an object already has a property with the specified name while calling the `Reflect.defineProperty()` method, the `Object.defineProperty()` method, or the `Object.defineProperties()` method, then the property is modified. The attributes that are not specified in the descriptor remain the same.

You can change a data property to an accessor property, and vice versa. If you do this, the configurable and enumerable attributes that are not specified in the descriptor will be preserved in the property. Other attributes that are not specified in the descriptor are set to their default values.

Here is example code that demonstrates how to create a data property using the `Reflect.defineProperty()` method:

```
var obj = {}
Reflect.defineProperty(obj, "name", {
  value: "Eden",
  writable: true,
  configurable: true,
  enumerable: true
});
console.log(obj.name); //Output "Eden"
```

Here is more example code that demonstrates how to create an accessor property using the `Reflect.defineProperty()` method:

```
var obj = { __name__: "Eden" }
Reflect.defineProperty(obj, "name", {
  get: function(){
    return this.__name__;
  },
  set: function(newName){
    this.__name__ = newName;
  },
  configurable: true,
  enumerable: true
});
obj.name = "John";
console.log(obj.name); //Output "John"
```

The Reflect.deleteProperty(object, property) method

The `Reflect.deleteProperty()` method is used to delete a property of an object. It's the same as the `delete` operator.

This method takes two arguments--that is, the first argument is the reference to the object and the second argument is the name of the property to delete. The `Reflect.deleteProperty()` method returns `true` if it has deleted the property successfully. Otherwise, it returns `false`.

Here is a code example that demonstrates how to delete a property using the `Reflect.deleteProperty()` method:

```
var obj = { name: "Eden" }
console.log(obj.name); //Output "Eden"
Reflect.deleteProperty(obj, "name");
console.log(obj.name); //Output "undefined"
```

The Reflect.get(object, property, this) method

The `Reflect.get()` method is used to retrieve the value of an object's property. The first argument is the object and the second argument is the property name. If the property is an accessor property, then we can provide a third argument, which will be the value of `this` inside the `get` function.

Here is a code example that demonstrates how to use the `Reflect.get()` method:

```
var obj = { __name__: "Eden" };
Reflect.defineProperty(obj, "name", {
  get: function(){
    return this.__name__;
  }
});
console.log(obj.name); //Output "Eden"
var name = Reflect.get(obj, "name", {__name__: "John"});
console.log(name); //Output "John"
```

The Reflect.set(object, property, value, this) method

The `Reflect.set()` method is used to set the value of an object's property. The first argument is the object, the second argument is the property name, and the third argument is the property value. If the property is an accessor property, then we can provide a fourth argument, which will be the value of `this` inside the `set` function.

The `Reflect.set()` method returns `true` if the property value was set successfully. Otherwise, it returns `false`.

Here is a code example that demonstrates how to use the `Reflect.set()` method:

```
var obj1 = { __name__: "Eden" };
Reflect.defineProperty(obj1, "name", {
  set: function(newName){
    this.__name__ = newName;
  },
  get: function(){
    return this.__name__;
  }
});
var obj2 = { __name__: "John" };
Reflect.set(obj1, "name", "Eden", obj2);
console.log(obj1.name); //Output "Eden"
console.log(obj2.__name__); //Output "Eden"
```

The Reflect.getOwnPropertyDescriptor(object, property) method

The `Reflect.getOwnPropertyDescriptor()` method is used to retrieve the descriptor of an object's property.

The `Reflect.getOwnPropertyDescriptor()` method is the same as the `Object.getOwnPropertyDescriptor()` method. The `Reflect.getOwnPropertyDescriptor()` method takes two arguments. The first argument is the object and the second argument is the property name.

Here is an example to demonstrate the `Reflect.getOwnPropertyDescriptor()` method:

```
var obj = { name: "Eden" };
var descriptor = Reflect.getOwnPropertyDescriptor(obj, "name");
console.log(descriptor.value);
console.log(descriptor.writable);
console.log(descriptor.enumerable);
console.log(descriptor.configurable);
```

The output is the following:

```
Eden
true
true
true
```

The Reflect.getPrototypeOf(object) method

The `Reflect.getPrototypeOf()` method is used to retrieve the prototype of an object--that is, the value of the internal `[[prototype]]` property of an object.

The `Reflect.getPrototypeOf()` method is the same as the `Object.getPrototypeOf()` method.

Here is a code example that demonstrates how to use the `Reflect. getPrototypeOf()` method:

```
var obj1 = {
__proto__:  { name: "Eden" }
};
var obj2 = Reflect.getPrototypeOf(obj1);
console.log(obj2.name); //Output "Eden"
```

The Reflect.setPrototypeOf(object, prototype) method

The `Reflect.setPrototypeOf()` is used to set the internal `[[prototype]]` property's value of an object. The `Reflect.setPrototypeOf()` method will return `true` if the internal `[[prototype]]` property's value was set successfully. Otherwise, it will return `false`.

Here is a code example that demonstrates how to use it:

```
var obj = {};
Reflect.setPrototypeOf(obj, { name: "Eden" });
console.log(obj.name); //Output "Eden"
```

The Reflect.has(object, property) method

The `Reflect.has()` is used to check if a property exists in an object. It also checks for the inherited properties. It returns `true` if the property exists. Otherwise, it returns `false`.

It's the same as the `in` operator in JavaScript.

Here is a code example that demonstrates how to use the Reflect.has() method:

```
var obj = {
  __proto__: { name: "Eden" },
  age: 12
};
console.log(Reflect.has(obj, "name")); //Output "true"
console.log(Reflect.has(obj, "age")); //Output "true"
```

The Reflect.isExtensible(object) method

The Reflect.isExtensible() method is used to check if an object is extensible or not,--that is, if we can add new properties to an object.

An object can be marked as non-extensible using the Object.preventExtensions(), Object.freeze(), and the Object.seal() methods.

The Reflect.isExtensible() method is the same as the Object.isExtensible() method.

Here is a code example that demonstrates how to use the Reflect.isExtensible() method:

```
var obj = { name: "Eden" };
console.log(Reflect.isExtensible(obj)); //Output "true"
Object.preventExtensions(obj);
console.log(Reflect.isExtensible(obj)); //Output "false"
```

The Reflect.preventExtensions(object) method

The Reflect.preventExtensions() is used to mark an object as non-extensible. It returns a Boolean, indicating whether the operation was successful or not.

It's the same as the Object.preventExtensions() method:

```
var obj = { name: "Eden" };
console.log(Reflect.isExtensible(obj)); //Output "true"
console.log(Reflect.preventExtensions(obj)); //Output "true"
console.log(Reflect.isExtensible(obj)); //Output "false"
```

The Reflect.ownKeys(object) method

The `Reflect.ownKeys()` method returns an array whose values represent the keys of the properties of a provided object. It ignores the inherited properties.

Here is the example code to demonstrate this method:

```
var obj = { a: 1, b: 2, __proto__: { c: 3 } };
var keys = Reflect.ownKeys(obj);
console.log(keys.length); //Output "2"
console.log(keys[0]); //Output "a"
console.log(keys[1]); //Output "b"
```

Summary

In this chapter, we learned what object reflection is and how to use the Reflect API for object reflection. We saw various methods of the `Reflect` object with examples. Overall, this chapter introduced the Reflect API to inspect and manipulate the properties of objects. In the next chapter, we will learn about proxies and their uses.

7
Proxies

Proxies are used to define the custom behavior of the fundamental operations on objects. Proxies are already available in programming languages such as C#, C++, and Java, but JavaScript has never had proxies. ES6 introduced the Proxy API, which lets us create proxies. In this chapter, we will look at proxies, their usage, and proxy traps. Due to the benefits of proxies, developers are using them increasingly and, therefore, it's important to learn about proxies in depth, with examples, which we will do in this chapter.

In this chapter, we'll cover:

- Creating proxies using the Proxy API
- Understanding what proxies are and how to use them
- Intercepting various operations on the objects using traps
- The different kinds of available traps
- Some use cases of proxies

Proxies in a nutshell

A proxy acts like a wrapper for an object and defines the custom behavior for the fundamental operations on the object. Some fundamental operations on the objects are property lookup, property assignment, constructor invocation, enumeration, and so on.

Think of it as a basic way of intercepting the operation you do with an object and its associated properties. For example, calling out a property value by writing `<objectname>.propertyName` should technically just echo out the property value, right?

What if you want to take a step back and inject your control right before the echoing part, but right after the calling part? Here's where proxies come in.

Once an object is wrapped using a proxy, all the operations that are supposed to be done on the object should now be done on the proxy object, so that the custom behavior can take place.

Terminology for proxies

Here are some important terms that are used while studying proxies:

- **Target:** This is the object that is wrapped by a proxy.
- **Traps:** These are functions that intercept various operations on the `target` object, and define the custom behavior for those operations.
- **Handler:** This is an object that holds the traps. A handler is attached to a proxy object.

Working with the Proxy API

The ES6 Proxy API provides the proxy constructor to create proxies. The proxy constructor takes two arguments, which are:

- **Target:** This is the object that will be wrapped by the proxy
- **Handler:** This is an object that contains the traps for the `target` object

A trap can be defined for every possible operation on the `target` object. If a trap is not defined, then the default action takes place on the target. Here is a code example that shows how to create a proxy, and does various operations on the `target` object. In this example, we have not defined any traps:

```
const target = {  age: 12 };
const handler = {};
const proxy = new Proxy(target, handler);
proxy.name = "Eden";
console.log(target.name);
console.log(proxy.name);
console.log(target.age);
console.log(proxy.age);
```

This outputs the following:

```
Eden
Eden
12
12
```

Here, we can see that the age property of the `target` object can be accessed via the `proxy` object. When we added the name property to the `proxy` object, it was actually added to the `target` object.

As there was no trap attached to the property assignment, the `proxy.name` assignment resulted in the default behavior--that is, simply assigning the value to the property.

So, we can say that a proxy is just a wrapper for a `target` object, and traps can be defined to change the default behavior of operations.

Many developers don't keep a reference variable for the `target` object, so use of the proxy is not mandatory for accessing the object. Keep a reference for the handler only when you need to reuse it for multiple proxies. Here is how to rewrite the previous code:

```
var proxy = new Proxy({ age: 12 }, {});
proxy.name = "Eden";
```

Proxy traps

There are different traps for the different operations that can be performed on an object. Some of the traps need to return values. There are some rules you need to follow when returning values. The returned values are intercepted by the proxy to filter and/or check if the returned values obey the rules. If a trap doesn't obey rules while returning a value, then the proxy throws the `TypeError` exception.

The value of `this` inside a trap is always a reference to the handler.

Let's take a look at the various kinds of traps.

The get(target, property, receiver) method

The get trap is executed when we retrieve a property value using the dot or bracket notation, or the `Reflect.get()` method. It takes three parameters--that is, the `target` object, the property name, and the proxy.

It must return a value that represents the property value. Here is a code example, which shows how to use the get trap:

```
const proxy = new Proxy({
    age: 12
}, {
get(target, property, receiver) {
    if(property in target) {
        return target[property];
    }
    return "Property not found!";
}
});
console.log(proxy.age);
console.log(proxy.name);
```

The output, as you might've figured out, is as follows:

```
12
Property not found!
```

Instead of the output, you will get the following without proxies:

```
12
undefined
```

Here, we can see that the get trap looks for the property in the `target` object and, if it finds it, then returns the `property` value. Otherwise, it returns a string indicating that it was not found.

The receiver parameter is the reference of the object whose property we intend to access. Consider this example to better understand the value of the receiver parameter:

```
const proxy = new Proxy({
    age: 13
}, {
get(target, property, receiver) {
    if(property in target) {
        return target[property];
    } else if(property == "name") {
        console.log("Receiver here is ", receiver);
        return "backup property value for name.";
    } else {
        return console.log("Property Not Found ", receiver);
    }
}
});
```

```
let temp = proxy.name;
let obj = {
    age: 12,
    __proto__: proxy
};
temp = obj.name;
const justARandomVariablePassingBy = obj.age;
console.log(justARandomVariablePassingBy);
```

The output:

```
Receiver here is <ProxyObject> {age: 13}
Receiver here is {age: 12}
12
```

Note that `{age: 13}` here is `ProxyObject`, `{ age: 12 }` is the normal object.

Here `obj` inherits the `proxy` object. Therefore, when the name property was not found in the `obj` object, it was searched for in the `proxy` object. As the `proxy` object had a get trap, it provided a value.

So, the value of the receiver parameter when we access the name property via the `obj.name` expression is `obj`, and when we access the name property via `proxy.name` the expression is `proxy`.

The value of the receiver parameter is decided in the same way for all other traps also.

Rules for using get trap

These rules shouldn't be violated when using the get trap:

- The value returned for a property must be the same as the value of the `target` object property if the `target` object property is a non-writable, non-configurable data property.
- The value returned for a property must be `undefined` if the `target` object property is a non-configurable accessor property that has `undefined` as its [[Get]] attribute.

The set(target, property, value, receiver) method

The set trap is invoked when we set the value of a property using the assignment operator, or the `Reflect.set()` method. It takes four parameter-- that is, the `target` object, the property name, the new property value, and the receiver.

The set trap must return `true` if the assignment was successful. Otherwise, it will return `false`.

Here is a code example that demonstrates how to use the set trap:

```
const proxy = new Proxy({}, {
set(target, property, value, receiver) {
    target[property] = value;
    return true;
}
});
proxy.name = "Eden";
console.log(proxy.name); //Output "Eden"
```

Rules for using set trap

These rules shouldn't be violated when using the set trap:

- If the `target` object property is a non-writable, non-configurable data property, then it will return as `false`--that is, you cannot change the property value
- If the `target` object property is a non-configurable accessor property that has `undefined` as its [[Set]] attribute, then it will return as `false`--that is, you cannot change the property value

The has(target, property) method

The has trap is executed when we check if a property exists or not, using the `in` operator. It takes two parameters--that is, the `target` object and the property name. It must return a Boolean value that indicates whether the property exists or not.

Here is a code example that demonstrates how to use the has trap:

```
const proxy = new Proxy({age: 12}, {
has(target, property) {
    return property in target;
}
});
console.log(Reflect.has(proxy, "name"));
console.log(Reflect.has(proxy, "age"));
```

The output is as follows:

```
false
true
```

Rules for using has trap

These rules shouldn't be violated when using the has trap:

- You cannot return `false` if the property exists as a non-configurable and is its own property of the `target` object
- You cannot return `false` if the property exists as an own property of the `target` object and the `target` object is not-extensible

The isExtensible(target) method

The `isExtensible` trap is executed when we check if the object is extensible or not, using the `Object.isExtensible()` method. It takes only one parameter--that is, the `target` object. It must return a Boolean value indicating whether the object is extensible or not.

Here is a code example that demonstrates how to use the `isExtensible` trap:

```
const proxy = new Proxy({age: 12}, {
isExtensible(target) {
    return Object.isExtensible(target);
}
});
console.log(Reflect.isExtensible(proxy)); //Output "true"
```

Rule for using isExtensible trap

This rule shouldn't be violated when using the `isExtensible` trap:

- You cannot return `false` if the target is extensible. Similarly, you cannot return `true` if the target is non-extensible

The getPrototypeOf(target) method

The `getPrototypeOf` trap is executed when we retrieve the value of the internal [[prototype]] property, using either the `Object.getPrototypeOf()` method or the `__proto__` property. It takes only one parameter--that is, the `target` object.

It must return an object or null value. The null value indicates that the object doesn't inherit anything else and is the end of the inheritance chain.

Here is a code example that demonstrates how to use the `getPrototypeOf` trap:

```
const proxy = new Proxy({
    age: 12,
    __proto__: {name: "Eden"}
},
{
    getPrototypeOf(target) {
        return Object.getPrototypeOf(target);
    }
});

console.log(Reflect.getPrototypeOf(proxy).name); //Output "Eden"
```

Rules for using getPrototypeOf trap

These rules shouldn't be violated when using the `getPrototypeOf` trap:

- It must either return an object or return a null value
- If the target is not-extensible, then this trap must return the actual prototype

The setPrototypeOf(target, prototype) method

The `setPrototypeOf` trap is executed when we set the value of the internal [[prototype]] property, using either the `Object.setPrototypeOf()` method or the `__proto__` property. It takes two parameters--that is, the `target` object and value of the property to be assigned.

This trap will return a Boolean, indicating whether it has successfully set the prototype or not.

Here is a code example that demonstrates how to use the `setPrototypeOf` trap:

```
const proxy = new Proxy({}, {
    setPrototypeOf(target, value) {
        Reflect.setPrototypeOf(target, value);
        return true;
    }
});

Reflect.setPrototypeOf(proxy, {name: "Eden"});
console.log(Reflect.getPrototypeOf(proxy).name); //Output "Eden"
```

Rule for using setPrototypeOf trap

This rule shouldn't be violated when using the `setPrototypeOf` trap:

- You must return `false` if the target is not-extensible

The preventExtensions(target) method

The `preventExtensions` trap is executed when we prevent the addition of new properties using the `Object.preventExtensions()` method. It takes only one parameter--that is, the `target` object.

It must return a Boolean, indicating whether it has successfully prevented the extension of the object or not.

Here is a code example that demonstrates how to use the `preventExtensions` trap:

```
const proxy = new Proxy({}, {
preventExtensions(target) {
    Object.preventExtensions(target);
    return true;
}
});
Reflect.preventExtensions(proxy);
proxy.a = 12;
console.log(proxy.a); //Output "undefined"
```

Rule for using preventExtensions trap

This rule shouldn't be violated when using the `preventExtensions` trap:

- This trap can return `true` only if the target is non-extensible or it has made the target non-extensible

The getOwnPropertyDescriptor(target, property) method

The `getOwnPropertyDescriptor` trap is executed when we retrieve the descriptor of a property by using the `Object.getOwnPropertyDescriptor()` method. It takes two parameters--that is, the `target` object and the name of the property.

This trap must return a `descriptor` object or `undefined`. The `undefined` value is returned if the property doesn't exist.

Here is a code example that demonstrates how to use the `getOwnPropertyDescriptor` trap:

```
const proxy = new Proxy({age: 12}, {
getOwnPropertyDescriptor(target, property) {
    return Object.getOwnPropertyDescriptor(target, property);
}
});

const descriptor = Reflect.getOwnPropertyDescriptor(proxy, "age");
console.log("Enumerable: " + descriptor.enumerable);
console.log("Writable: " + descriptor.writable);
console.log("Configurable: " + descriptor.configurable);
console.log("Value: " + descriptor.value);
```

The output is as follows:

```
Enumerable: true
Writable: true
Configurable: true
Value: 12
```

Rules for using getOwnPropertyDescriptor trap

These rules shouldn't be violated when using the `getOwnPropertyDescriptor` trap:

- This trap must either return an object or return an `undefined` property
- You cannot return the `undefined` value if the property exists as a non-configurable own property of the `target` object
- You cannot return the `undefined` value if the property exists as an own property of the `target` object and the `target` object is not-extensible
- You will have to return `undefined` if the property does not exist as an own property of the `target` object and the `target` object is not-extensible
- You cannot make the configurable property of the returned descriptor object `false` if the property exists as an own property of the `target` object, or if it exists as a configurable own property of the `target` object

The defineProperty(target, property, descriptor) method

The `defineProperty` trap is executed when we define a property using the `Object.defineProperty()` method. It takes three parameters--that is, the `target` object, the property name, and the `descriptor` object.

This trap should return a Boolean indicating whether it has successfully defined the property or not.

Here is a code example that demonstrates how to use the `defineProperty` trap:

```
const proxy = new Proxy({}, {
defineProperty(target, property, descriptor) {
    Object.defineProperty(target, property, descriptor);
    return true;
}
});
Reflect.defineProperty(proxy, "name", {value: "Eden"});
console.log(proxy.name); //Output "Eden"
```

Rule for using defineProperty

This rule shouldn't be violated when using the `defineProperty` trap:

- It must return `false` if the `target` object is not-extensible, and the property doesn't yet exist

The deleteProperty(target, property) method

The `deleteProperty` trap is executed when we delete a property using either the delete operator or the `Reflect.deleteProperty()` method. It takes two parameters--that is, the `target` object and the property name.

This trap must return a Boolean, indicating whether the property was deleted successfully or not. Here is a code example that demonstrates how to use the `deleteProperty` trap:

```
const proxy = new Proxy({age: 12}, {
deleteProperty(target, property) {
    return delete target[property];
}
});
Reflect.deleteProperty(proxy, "age");
console.log(proxy.age); //Output "undefined"
```

Rule for deleteProperty trap

This rule shouldn't be violated when using the `deleteProperty` trap:

- This trap must return `false` if the property exists as a non-configurable own property of the `target` object

The ownKeys(target) method

The `ownKeys` trap is executed when we retrieve the own property keys using the `Reflect.ownKeys()`, `Object.getOwnPropertyNames()`, `Object.getOwnPropertySymbols()` and the `Object.keys()` methods. It takes only one parameter--that is, the `target` object.

The `Reflect.ownKeys()` method is similar to the `Object.getOwnPropertyNames()` method--that is, they both return the enumerable and non-enumerable property keys of an object.

They also both ignore the inherited properties. The only difference is that the `Reflect.ownKeys()` method returns both the symbol and string keys, whereas the `Object.getOwnPropertyNames()` method returns only the string keys.

The `Object.getOwnPropertySymbols()` method returns the enumerable and non-enumerable properties whose keys are symbols. It ignores the inherited properties.

The `Object.keys()` method is similar to the `Object.getOwnPropertyNames()` method, but the only difference is that the `Object.keys()` method returns the enumerable properties only.

The `ownKeys` trap must return an array, representing the own property keys.

Here is a code example which demonstrates how to use the `ownKeys` trap:

```
const s = Symbol();
const object = {age: 12, __proto__: {name: "Eden"}, [s]: "Symbol"};
Object.defineProperty(object, "profession",
{
    enumerable: false,
    configurable: false,
    writable: false,
    value: "Developer"
})
```

```
const proxy = new Proxy(object, {
    ownKeys(target) {
        return
Object.getOwnPropertyNames(target).concat(Object.getOwnPropertySymbols(targ
et));
}
});

console.log(Reflect.ownKeys(proxy));
console.log(Object.getOwnPropertyNames(proxy));
console.log(Object.keys(proxy));
console.log(Object.getOwnPropertySymbols(proxy));
```

The output is as follows:

```
["age", "profession", Symbol()]
["age", "profession"]
["age"]
[Symbol()]
```

Here, we can see that the values of the array returned by the `ownKeys` trap are filtered by the proxy, based on what the caller expected. For example, the `Object.getOwnPropertySymbols()` caller expected an array of symbols. Therefore, the proxy removed the strings from the returned array.

Rules for using ownKeys trap

These rules shouldn't be violated when using the `ownKeys` trap:

- The elements of the returned array must either be a string or symbol
- The returned array must contain the keys of all the non-configurable own properties of the `target` object
- If the `target` object is not-extensible, then the returned array must contain all the keys of the own properties and of the `target` object, and no other values

The apply(target, thisValue, arguments) method

If the target is a function, then calling the proxy will execute the `apply` trap. The `apply` trap is also executed for the function's `apply()` and `call()` methods, and the `Reflect.apply()` method.

The apply trap takes three parameters. The first parameter is the `target` object and the third parameter is an array, representing the arguments of the function call.

The second parameter is the same as the value of `this` of the `target` function--that is, it's the same as the value of `this` of the target function if the target function would have been invoked without the proxy.

Here is a code example that demonstrates how to use the apply trap:

```
const proxy = new Proxy(function(){}, {
    apply(target, thisValue, arguments) {
        console.log(thisValue.name);
        return arguments[0] + arguments[1] + arguments[2];
    }
});

const obj = { name: "Eden", f: proxy }
const sum = obj.f(1,2,3);
console.log(sum);
```

The output is as follows:

```
Eden
6
```

The construct(target, arguments) method

If the target is a function, then calling the target as a constructor using the `new` operator or the `Reflect.construct()` method will execute the construct trap.

The construct trap takes two parameters. The first parameter is the `target` object and the second parameter is an array, representing the arguments of the constructor call.

The `construct` trap must return an object, representing the newly created instance. Here is a code example that demonstrates how to use the `construct` trap:

```
const proxy = new Proxy(function(){}, {
    construct(target, arguments) {
        return {name: arguments[0]};
    }
});

const obj = new proxy("Eden");
console.log(obj.name); //Output "Eden"
```

The Proxy.revocable(target, handler) method

A revocable proxy is a proxy that can be revoked (that is, switched off).

To create revocable proxies we have to use the `Proxy.revocable()` method. The `Proxy.revocable()` method is not a constructor. This method also takes the same arguments as the `Proxy` constructor, but, instead of returning a revocable proxy instance directly, it returns an object with two properties, which are the following:

- `proxy`: This is the revocable `proxy` object
- `revoke`: When this function is called, it revokes the proxy

Once a revocable `proxy` is revoked, any attempts to use it will throw a `TypeError` exception. Here is an example to demonstrate how to create a revocable `proxy` and `revoke` it:

```
const revocableProxy = Proxy.revocable({ age: 12 }, {
get(target, property, receiver) {
    if(property in target) {
        return target[property];
    }
    return "Not Found";
}
});
console.log(revocableProxy.proxy.age);
revocableProxy.revoke();
console.log(revocableProxy.proxy.name);
```

The output is as follows:

```
12
TypeError: proxy is revoked
```

Use case of revocable proxy

You can use the revocable proxies instead of the regular proxies. You can use it when you pass a proxy to a function that runs asynchronously or in parallel, so that you can revoke it when you don't want the function to be able to use that proxy anymore.

The uses of proxies

There are several uses of proxies. Here are some main use cases:

- Creating virtualized objects, such as remote objects, persistent objects, and more
- The lazy creation of objects
- Transparent logging, tracing, profiling, and more
- Embedded domain specific languages
- Generically interposing abstractions in order to enforce access control

Summary

In this chapter, we learned what proxies are and how to use them. We saw the various traps available with examples. We also saw different rules that need to be followed by different traps. This chapter explained everything about the Proxy API in JavaScript in depth. Finally, we saw some use cases of proxies. In the next chapter, we will walk through object-oriented programming and the ES6 classes.

8
Classes

JavaScript has classes that provide a much simpler and clearer syntax for creating constructors and dealing with inheritance. Until now, JavaScript never had the concept of classes, although it's an object-oriented programming language. Programmers from other programming language backgrounds often found it difficult to understand JavaScript's object-oriented model and inheritance due to the lack of classes.

In this chapter, we will learn about object-oriented JavaScript using classes:

- JavaScript data types
- Creating objects the classical way
- The constructors of the primitive types
- What are classes?
- Creating objects using classes
- Inheritance in classes
- The features of classes

Understanding object-oriented JavaScript

Before we proceed with ES6 classes, let's refresh our knowledge of JavaScript data types, constructors, and inheritance. While learning classes, we will be comparing the syntax of constructors and prototype-based inheritance with the syntax of classes. Therefore, it is important to have a good grasp of these topics.

The JavaScript data types

JavaScript variables hold (or store) data (or values). The type of data variables that they hold is called the data type. In JavaScript, there are seven different data types: number, string, Boolean, null, undefined, symbol, and object.

When it comes to holding objects, variables hold the object reference (that is, the memory address) instead of the object itself. If you're coming from a C/C++ background, you can relate them to pointers, but not exactly.

All data types other than objects are called primitive data types.

The arrays and functions are actually the JavaScript objects. A lot of things are objects under the hood.

Creating objects

There are two ways of creating an object in JavaScript: using the `object` literal, or using a `constructor`. The `object` literal is used when we want to create fixed objects, whereas a `constructor` is used when we want to create objects dynamically at runtime.

Let's consider a case where we may need to use the `constructor` instead of the `object` literal. Here is a code example:

```
const student = {
    name: "Eden",
    printName() {
        console.log(this.name);
    }
}
student.printName(); //Output "Eden"
```

Here, we created a `student` object using the `object` literal, that is, the `{}` notation. This works well when you just want to create a single `student` object.

But the problem arises when you want to create multiple `student` objects. Obviously, you don't want to write the previous code multiple times to create multiple `student` objects. This is where `constructor` comes into use.

A `function` acts like a `constructor` when invoked using the `new` keyword. A `constructor` creates and returns an object. The `this` keyword inside a `function`, when invoked as a `constructor`, points to the new object instance, and once the `constructor` execution is finished, the new object is automatically returned. Consider this example:

```
function Student(name) {
    this.name = name;
}

Student.prototype.printName = function(){
    console.log(this.name);
}

const student1 = new Student("Eden");
const student2 = new Student("John");
student1.printName(); //Output "Eden"
student2.printName(); //Output "John"
```

Here, to create multiple `student` objects, we invoked the `constructor` multiple times instead of creating multiple `student` objects using the `object` literals.

To add methods to the instances of the `constructor`, we didn't use the `this` keyword; instead, we used the `prototype` property of `constructor`. We will learn more about why we did it this way, and what the `prototype` property is, in the next section.

Actually, every object must belong to a `constructor`. Every object has an inherited property named `constructor`, pointing to the object's `constructor`. When we create objects using the `object` literal, the `constructor` property points to the global `Object` of the `constructor`. Consider this example to understand this behavior:

```
var student = {}
console.log(student.constructor == Object); //Output "true"
```

Understanding the prototypal inheritance model

Each JavaScript object has an internal `[[prototype]]` property pointing to another object called its prototype. This prototype object has a prototype of its own, and so on, until an object is reached with null as its prototype. null has no prototype, and it acts as a final link in the prototype chain.

When trying to access a property of an object, and if the property is not found in the object, then the property is searched for in the object's prototype. If still not found, then it's searched for in the prototype of the prototype object. It keeps on going until null is encountered in the prototype chain. This is how inheritance works in JavaScript.

As a JavaScript object can have only one prototype, JavaScript supports only a single inheritance.

While creating objects using the `object` literal, we can use the special `__proto__` property or the `Object.setPrototypeOf()` method to assign a prototype of an object. JavaScript also provides an `Object.create()` method, with which we can create a new object with a specified prototype, as `__proto__` lacks browser support, and the `Object.setPrototypeOf()` method seems a little odd.

Here is a code example that demonstrates different ways to set the prototype of an object while creating that particular object using the `Object` literal:

```
const object1 = { name: "Eden", __proto__: {age: 24} }
const object2 = {name: "Eden" }

Object.setPrototypeOf(object2, {age: 24});

const object3 = Object.create({age: 24}, {
    name: {value: "Eden"}
});

console.log(object1.name + " " + object1.age);
console.log(object2.name + " " + object2.age);
console.log(object3.name + " " + object3.age);
```

The output is as follows:

```
Eden 24
Eden 24
Eden 24
```

Here, the `{age:24}` object is referred to as a base object, super object, or parent object as it's being inherited. And the `{name:"Eden"}` object is referred to as the derived object, subobject, or the child object, as it inherits another object.

If you don't assign a prototype to an object while creating it using the `object` literal, then the prototype points to the `Object.prototype` property. The prototype of `Object.prototype` is null, therefore leading to the end of the prototype chain. Here is an example to demonstrate this:

```
const obj = { name: "Eden" }
console.log(obj.__proto__ == Object.prototype); //Output "true"
```

While creating objects using a `constructor`, the prototype of the new objects always points to a property named prototype of the `function` object. By default, the `prototype` property is an object with one property named the `constructor`. The `constructor` property points to the `function` itself. Consider this example to understand this model:

```
function Student() {
    this.name = "Eden";
}
const obj = new Student();
console.log(obj.__proto__.constructor == Student); //Output "true"
console.log(obj.__proto__ == Student.prototype); //Output "true"
```

To add new methods to the instances of a `constructor`, we should add them to the `prototype` property of the `constructor`, as we did earlier.

The reason why we didn't add the methods to the `constructor` using `this` previously is that every instance of the `constructor` will have a copy of the methods, and this isn't very memory-efficient. By attaching methods to the `prototype` property of a `constructor`, there is only one copy of each function that all the instances share. To understand this, consider this example:

```
function Student(name) {
    this.name = name;
}
Student.prototype.printName = function() {
    console.log(this.name);
}

const s1 = new Student("Eden");
const s2 = new Student("John");

function School(name) {
    this.name = name;
    this.printName = function() {
        console.log(this.name);
    }
}
```

```
const s3 = new School("ABC");
const s4 = new School("XYZ");
console.log(s1.printName == s2.printName);
console.log(s3.printName == s4.printName);
```

The output is as follows:

```
true
false
```

Here, `s1` and `s2` share the same `printName` function that reduces the use of memory, whereas `s3` and `s4` contain two different functions called `printName` that make the program use more memory. This is unnecessary, as both the functions do the same thing. Therefore, we add methods for the instances to the `prototype` property of the `constructor`.

Implementing the inheritance hierarchy in the `constructor` is not as straightforward as for `object` literals. This is because the child `constructor` needs to invoke the parent `constructor` for the parent constructor's initialization logic to take place, and we need to add the methods of the `prototype` property of the parent `constructor` to the `prototype` property of the child `constructor` so that we can use them with the objects of the child `constructor`. There is no predefined way to do all this. Developers and JavaScript libraries have their own ways of doing this. I will show you the most common way of doing it.

Here is an example to demonstrate how to implement inheritance while creating objects using the constructors:

```
function School(schoolName) {
    this.schoolName = schoolName;
}

School.prototype.printSchoolName = function(){
    console.log(this.schoolName);
}

function Student(studentName, schoolName) {
    this.studentName = studentName;
    School.call(this, schoolName);
}

Student.prototype = new School();
Student.prototype.printStudentName = function() {
    console.log(this.studentName);
}
```

```
const s = new Student("Eden", "ABC School");
s.printStudentName();
s.printSchoolName();
```

The output is as follows:

```
Eden
ABC School
```

Here, we invoked the parent `constructor` using the `call` method of the `function` object. To inherit the methods, we created an instance of the parent `constructor` and assigned it to the child constructor's `prototype` property.

This is not a foolproof way of implementing inheritance in the constructors, as there are lots of potential problems. For example, if the parent `constructor` does something other than just initialize properties, such as DOM manipulation, then assigning a new instance of the parent `constructor` to the `prototype` property of the child `constructor` can cause problems.

Therefore, classes provide a better and easier way to inherit existing constructors and classes. We will see more on this later in this chapter.

The constructors of primitive data types

Primitive data types, such as Boolean, string, and number, have their constructor counterparts. These counterpart constructors behave like wrappers for these primitive types. For example, the `String` constructor is used to create a string object that contains an internal `[[PrimitiveValue]]` property that holds the actual primitive value.

At runtime, wherever necessary, the primitive values are wrapped with their `constructor` counterparts, and the counterpart objects are treated as primitive values so that the code works as expected. Consider this example code to understand how it works:

```
const s1 = "String";
const s2 = new String("String");
console.log(typeof s1);
console.log(typeof s2);
console.log(s1 == s2);
console.log(s1.length);
```

The output is as follows:

```
string
object
true
6
```

Here, `s1` is a primitive type, and `s2` is an object although applying the == operator on them gives us a true result. s1 is a primitive type but still we are able to access the length property even though primitive types shouldn't have any properties.

All this is happening because the previous code was converted into this at run-time:

```
const s1 = "String";
const s2 = new String("String");

console.log(typeof s1);
console.log(typeof s2);
console.log(s1 == s2.valueOf());
console.log((new String(s1)).length);
```

Here, we can see how the primitive value was wrapped with its `constructor` counterpart, and how the object counterpart was treated as a primitive value where necessary. Therefore, the code works as expected.

Primitive types introduced from ES6 onwards won't allow their counterpart functions to be invoked as constructors, that is, we can't explicitly wrap them using their object counterparts. We saw this behavior while learning symbols.

The null and undefined primitive types don't have any counterpart constructors.

Using classes

We saw that JavaScript's object-oriented model is based on constructors and prototype-based inheritance. Well, ES6 classes are just a new syntax for the existing model. Classes do not introduce a new object-oriented model to JavaScript.

ES6 classes aim to provide a much simpler and clearer syntax for dealing with the constructors and inheritance.

In fact, classes are functions. Classes are just a new syntax for creating functions that are used as constructors. Creating functions using classes that aren't used as constructors doesn't make any sense, and offers no benefits.

Rather, it makes your code difficult to read, as it becomes confusing. Therefore, use classes only if you want to use them to construct objects. Let's have a look at classes in detail.

Defining a class

Just as there are two ways of defining functions, function declarations and function expressions, there are two ways to define a class: using the class declaration and the class expression.

The class declaration

To define a class using the `class` declaration, you need to use the `class` keyword and a name for the `class`.

Here is a code example to demonstrate how to define a class using the `class` declaration:

```
class Student {
    constructor(name) {
        this.name = name;
    }
}

const s1 = new Student("Eden");
console.log(s1.name); //Output "Eden"
```

Here, we created a `class` named `Student`. Then, we defined a `constructor` method in it. Finally, we created a new instance of the class—an object, and logged the name property of the object.

The body of a `class` is in the curly brackets, that is, `{}`. This is where we need to define methods. Methods are defined without the `function` keyword, and a comma is not used in between the methods.

Classes are treated as functions; internally the class name is treated as the function name, and the body of the `constructor` method is treated as the body of the function.

There can only be one `constructor` method in a `class`. Defining more than one `constructor` will throw the `SyntaxError` exception.

All the code inside a class body is executed in strict mode, by default.

The previous code is the same as this code when written using a `function`:

```
function Student(name) {
    this.name = name;
}

const s1 = new Student("Eden");
console.log(s1.name); //Output "Eden"
```

To prove that a `class` is a `function`, consider this code:

```
class Student {
    constructor(name) {
        this.name = name;
    }
}

function School(name) {
    this.name = name;
}

console.log(typeof Student);
console.log(typeof School == typeof Student);
```

The output is as follows:

```
function
true
```

Here, we can see that a `class` is a `function`. It's just a new syntax for creating a function.

The class expression

A class expression has a similar syntax to a `class` declaration. However, with `class` expressions, you are able to omit the class name. The body and behavior remain the same both ways.

Here is a code example to demonstrate how to define a `class` using a `class` expression:

```
const Student = class {
    constructor(name) {
        this.name = name;
    }
}

const s1 = new Student("Eden");
console.log(s1.name); //Output "Eden"
```

Here, we stored a reference of the `class` in a variable and used it to construct the objects.

The previous code is the same as this code when written using a `function`:

```
const Student = function(name) {
    this.name = name;
};
const s1 = new Student("Eden");
console.log(s1.name); //Output "Eden"
```

The prototype methods

All the methods in the body of the `class` are added to the `prototype` property of the class. The `prototype` property is the prototype of the objects created using `class`.

Here is an example that shows how to add methods to the `prototype` property of a `class`:

```
class Person {
    constructor(name, age) {
        this.name = name;
        this.age = age;
    }
    printProfile() {
        console.log("Name is: " + this.name + " and Age is: " + this.age);
    }
}

const p = new Person("Eden", 12);
p.printProfile();
console.log("printProfile" in p.__proto__);
console.log("printProfile" in Person.prototype);
```

The output is as follows:

```
Name is: Eden and Age is: 12
true
true
```

Here, we can see that the `printProfile` method was added to the `prototype` property of the `class`.

The previous code is the same as this code when written using a `function`:

```
function Person(name, age) {
    this.name = name;
    this.age = age;
}

Person.prototype.printProfile = function() {
    console.log("Name is: " + this.name + " and Age is: " + this.age);
}

const p = new Person("Eden", 12);
p.printProfile();
console.log("printProfile" in p.__proto__);
console.log("printProfile" in Person.prototype);
```

The output is as follows:

```
Name is: Eden and Age is: 12
true
true
```

Getters and setters

Earlier, to add accessor properties to objects we had to use the `Object.defineProperty()` method. From ES6 onwards, there are get and set prefixes for methods. These methods can be added to `object` literals and classes to define the get and set attributes of the accessor properties.

When get and `set` methods are used in a `class` body, they are added to the `prototype` property of the class.

Here is an example to demonstrate how to define the get and set methods in a class:

```
class Person {
    constructor(name) {
        this._name_ = name;
    }
    get name() {
        return this._name_;
    }
    set name(name) {
        this.someOtherCustomProp = true;
        this._name_ = name;
    }
}

const p = new Person("Eden");
console.log(p.name); // Outputs: "Eden"
p.name = "John";
console.log(p.name); // Outputs: "John"
console.log(p.someOtherCustomProp); // Outputs: "true"
```

Here, we created an accessor property to encapsulate the _name_ property. We also logged some other information to prove that name is an accessor property that is added to the prototype property of the class.

The generator method

To treat a concise method of an object literal as the generator method, or to treat a method of a class as the generator method, we can simply prefix it with the * character.

The generator method of a class is added to the prototype property of the class.

Here is an example to demonstrate how to define a generator method in the class:

```
class myClass {
    * generator_function() {
        yield 1;
        yield 2;
        yield 3;
        yield 4;
        yield 5;
    }
}

const obj = new myClass();
```

```
let generator = obj.generator_function();
console.log(generator.next().value);
console.log(generator.next().value);
console.log(generator.next().value);
console.log(generator.next().value);
console.log(generator.next().value);
console.log(generator.next().done);
console.log("generator_function" in myClass.prototype);
```

The output is as follows:

```
1
2
3
4
5
true
true
```

Static methods

The methods that are added to the body of the `class` with the `static` prefix are called `static` methods. The `static` methods are the class' own methods; that is, they are added to the class itself rather than the `prototype` property of the `class`. For example, the `String.fromCharCode()` method is a `static` method of the string `constructor`, that is, `fromCharCode` is the property of the `String` function itself.

The `static` methods are often used to create utility functions for an application.

Here is an example to demonstrate how to define and use a `static` method in a `class`:

```
class Student {
    constructor(name)  {
        this.name = name;
    }
    static findName(student)  {
        return student.name;
    }
}

const s = new Student("Eden");
const name = Student.findName(s);
console.log(name); //Output "Eden"
```

Implementing inheritance in classes

Earlier in this chapter, we saw how difficult it was to implement inheritance hierarchies in functions. Therefore, ES6 aims to make it easy by introducing the `extends` clause and the `super` keyword for classes.

By using the `extends` clause, a `class` can inherit static and non-static properties from another `constructor` (which may or may not be defined using a class).

The super keyword is used in two ways:

- It's used in a class `constructor` method to call the parent `constructor`
- When used inside the methods of a `class`, it references the static and non-static methods of the parent `constructor`

Here is an example to demonstrate how to implement an inheritance hierarchy in constructors using the `extends` clause, and the `super` keyword:

```
function A(a) {
    this.a = a;
}

A.prototype.printA = function(){
    console.log(this.a);
}

class B extends A {
    constructor(a, b)  {
        super(a);
        this.b = b;
    }
    printB()  {
        console.log(this.b);
    }

    static sayHello()  {
        console.log("Hello");
    }
}

class C extends B {
    constructor(a, b, c)  {
        super(a, b);
        this.c = c;
    }
```

```
        printC()  {
            console.log(this.c);
        }

        printAll()  {
            this.printC();
            super.printB();
            super.printA();
        }
    }

    const obj = new C(1, 2, 3);
    obj.printAll();
    C.sayHello();
```

The output is as follows:

```
3
2
1
Hello
```

Here, `A` is a function `constructor`; `B` is a `class` that inherits `A`; `C` is a `class` that inherits `B`; and as `B` inherits `A`, therefore `C` also inherits `A`.

As a class can inherit a function `constructor`, we can also inherit prebuilt function constructors, such as string and array, and also custom function constructors using the classes instead of the alternative hacky ways that we used to use.

The previous example also shows how and where to use the `super` keyword. Remember that, inside the `constructor` method, you need to use the `super` keyword before using the `this` keyword. Otherwise, an exception is thrown.

If a child class doesn't have a `constructor` method, then the default behavior will invoke the `constructor` method of the parent class.

Computed method names

You can also decide the name of static and non-static methods of a `class` and concise methods of an `object` literal at run-time; that is, you can define method name via expressions. Here is an example to demonstrate this:

```
    class myClass {
        static ["my" + "Method"]() {
```

```
        console.log("Hello");
    }
}

myClass["my" + "Method"](); //Output "Hello"
```

Computed property names also allow you to use symbols as keys for the methods. Here is an example to demonstrate this:

```
var s = Symbol("Sample");

class myClass {
    static [s]() {
        console.log("Hello");
    }
}

myClass[s](); //Output "Hello"
```

The attributes of properties

When using a class, the attributes of the static and non-static properties of the `constructor` are different from when declared using a function:

- The `static` methods are writable and configurable, but not enumerable
- The `prototype` property and the `prototype.constructor` property of a `class` are not writable, enumerable, or configurable
- The properties of the `prototype` property are writable and configurable, but not enumerable

Classes are not hoisted!

You can call a function before it's defined; that is, function calls can be made before the function definition. But, you cannot use a `class` before it's defined. Trying to do so in classes will throw the `ReferenceError` exception.

Here is an example to demonstrate this:

```
myFunc(); // fine
function myFunc(){}
var obj = new myClass(); // throws error
class myClass {}
```

Overriding the result of the constructor method

The `constructor` method, by default, returns the new instance if there is no return statement in it. If there is a return statement, then any value in the return statement is returned. This might seem a little weird if you're coming from a language like C++ as you cannot usually return any value from the `constructor` there.

Here is an example to demonstrate this:

```
class myClass {
    constructor() {
        return Object.create(null);
    }
}

console.log(new myClass() instanceof myClass); //Output "false"
```

The Symbol.species static accessor property

The `@@species` static accessor property is optionally added to a child `constructor` in order to notify the methods of the parent `constructor` about what the `constructor` should use if the parent constructor's methods are returning new instances. If the `@@species` static accessor property is not defined on a child `constructor`, then the methods of the parent `constructor` can use the default `constructor`.

Consider this example to understand the use of `@@species`—the `map()` method of the array objects returns a new Array instance. If we call the `map()` method of an object that inherits an `Array` object, then the `map()` method returns a new instance of the child `constructor` instead of the `Array` constructor, which is not what we always want. The `@@species` property, which provides a way to signal such kinds of functions, uses a different `constructor` instead of the default `constructor`.

Here is a code example to demonstrate how to use the `@@species` static accessor property:

```
class myCustomArray1 extends Array {
    static get [Symbol.species]()  {
        return Array;
    }
}

class myCustomArray2 extends Array{}

var arr1 = new myCustomArray1(0, 1, 2, 3, 4);
```

```
var arr2 = new myCustomArray2(0, 1, 2, 3, 4);

console.log(arr1 instanceof myCustomArray1); // Outputs "true"
console.log(arr2 instanceof myCustomArray2); // Outputs "true"
arr1 = arr1.map(value => value + 1);
arr2 = arr2.map(value => value + 1);

console.log(arr1 instanceof myCustomArray1);  // Outputs "false"
console.log(arr2 instanceof myCustomArray2);  // Outputs "true"
console.log(arr1 instanceof Array); // Outputs "true"
console.log(arr2 instanceof Array); // Outputs "true"
```

It is recommended that, if you are creating a JavaScript library, then the methods of the constructors in your library should always look for the `@@species` property while returning new instances. Here is an example to demonstrate this:

```
//Assume myArray1 is part of library
class myArray1 {
//default @@species. Child class will inherit this property
    static get [Symbol.species]() {
        //default constructor
        return this;
    }
    mapping() {
        return new this.constructor[Symbol.species]();
    }
}

class myArray2 extends myArray1 {
    static get [Symbol.species]() {
        return myArray1;
    }
}

let arr = new myArray2();
console.log(arr instanceof myArray2); //Output "true"
arr = arr.mapping();
console.log(arr instanceof myArray1); //Output "true"
```

If you don't want to define a default `@@species` property in parent constructors, then you can use the `if...else` conditional to check whether the `@@species` property is defined or not, but the previous pattern is preferred. The built-in `map()` method also uses the previous pattern.

All the built-in methods of the JavaScript constructors from ES6 look for a `@@species` property if they return a new instance. For example, the methods of `Array`, `Map`, `ArrayBuffer`, `Promise`, and other such constructors look for the `@@species` property if they return new instances.

The new.target implicit parameter

The default value of new.target is undefined, but when a function is invoked as a constructor, the value of the new.target parameter depends on the following conditions:

- If a constructor is invoked using a new operator, then new.target points to this constructor
- If a constructor is invoked via the super keyword, then the value of new.target in it is the same as the value of new.target of the constructor that is called super.

Inside an arrow function, the value of new.target is the same as the value for the `new.target` of the surrounding non-arrow function.

Here is example code to demonstrate this:

```
function myConstructor() {
    console.log(new.target.name);
}

class myClass extends myConstructor {
    constructor() {
        super();
    }
}

const obj1 = new myClass();
const obj2 = new myConstructor();
```

The output is as follows:

```
myClass
myConstructor
```

Using super in object literals

The super keyword can also be used in concise methods of object literals. The super keyword in concise methods of the object literals has the same value as the `[[prototype]]` property of the object defined by the object literal.

In object literals, super is used to access overridden properties by the child object.

Here is an example to demonstrate how to use super in object literals:

```
const obj1 = {
    print() {
        console.log("Hello");
    }
}

const obj2 = {
    print() {
        super.print();
    }
}

Object.setPrototypeOf(obj2, obj1);
obj2.print(); //Output "Hello"
```

ES.next proposal includes adding support for truly private properties in classes using the hash (#) symbol. #myProp inside a class will be private to that class.

Summary

In this chapter, we first learned the basics of Object-Oriented Programming using a traditional function approach. Then, we jumped to classes and learned how they make it easy for us to read and write object-oriented JavaScript code. We also learned about some miscellaneous features such as the `new.target` and accessor methods. Let us now move on to the web, a place where we can implement what we've learned so far!

9
JavaScript on the Web

Hello there! So far, we've learned and created a solid understanding of JavaScript, how it works under the hood, and what it contains. But how do we actually use it today? How do we start building something? This is the chapter that deals with this.

In this chapter, we'll learn about:

- HTML5 and the rise of modern JavaScript
- What is **Document Object Model** (**DOM**)?
- DOM methods/properties
- Modern JavaScript browser APIs
- Page Visibility API
- Navigator API
- Clipboard API
- Canvas API - the web's drawing board
- Fetch API

HTML5 and the rise of modern JavaScript

The HTML5 specification arrived in 2008. HTML5, however, was so technologically advanced in 2008 that it was predicted that it would not be ready till at least 2022! However, that turned out to be incorrect, and here we are, with fully supported HTML5 and ES6/ES7/ES8-supported browsers.

A lot of APIs used by HTML5 go hand in hand with JavaScript. Before looking at those APIs, let us understand a little about how JavaScript sees the web. This'll eventually put us in a strong position to understand various interesting, JavaScript-related things such as the Web Workers API, which deserves its own chapter (spoiler alert: It is included in this book!)

The HTML DOM

The HTML DOM is a tree version of how the document looks. Here is a very simple example of an HTML document:

```
<!doctype HTML>
<html>
    <head>
        <title>Cool Stuff!</title>
    </head>
    <body>
        <p>Awesome!</p>
    </body>
</html>
```

Here's how its tree version will look:

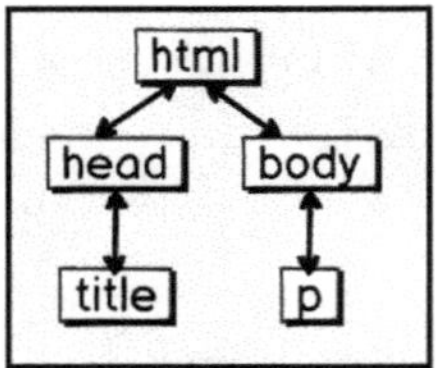

The previous diagram is just a rough representation of the DOM tree. HTML tags consist of **head** and **body**; furthermore, the `<body>` tag consists of a `<p>` tag, whereas the `<head>` tag consists of the `<title>` tag. Simple!

JavaScript has access to the DOM directly, and can modify the connections between these nodes, add nodes, remove nodes, change contents, attach event listeners, and so on.

What is the Document Object Model (DOM)?

Simply put, the DOM is a way to represent HTML or XML documents as nodes. This makes it easier for other programming languages to connect to a DOM-following page and modify it accordingly.

To be clear, DOM is not a programming language. DOM provides JavaScript with a way to interact with web pages. You can think of it as a standard. Every element is part of the DOM tree, which can be accessed and modified with APIs exposed to JavaScript.

DOM is not restricted to being accessed only by JavaScript. It is language-independent and there are several modules available in various languages to parse DOM (just like JavaScript) including PHP, Python, Java, and so on.

As said previously, DOM provides JavaScript with a way to interact with it. How? Well, accessing DOM is as easy as accessing predefined objects in JavaScript: `document`. The DOM API specifies what you'll find inside the `document` object. The `document` object essentially gives JavaScript access to the DOM tree formed by your HTML document. If you notice, you cannot access any element at all without actually accessing the `document` object first.

DOM methods/properties

All HTML elements are objects in JavaScript. The most commonly used object is the `document` object. It has the whole DOM tree attached to it. You can query for elements on that. Let's look at some very common examples of these methods:

- `getElementById` method
- `getElementsByTagName` method
- `getElementsByClassName` method
- `querySelector` method
- `querySelectorAll` method

By no means is this an exhaustive list of all methods available. However, this list should at least get you started with DOM manipulation. Use MDN as your reference for various other methods. Here's the link: `https://developer.mozilla.org/en-US/docs/Web/API/Document#Methods`.

Using the getElementById method

In HTML, you can assign an element an `ID` and then retrieve it back in JavaScript for manipulation. Here's how:

```
<div id="myID">My Content Here</div>
<script>
const myID = document.getElementById('myID'); // myID now contains
reference to the div above
</script>
```

Once you have that, you can access the properties of this object, which in turn actually modifies the element on the screen accordingly.

Using the getElementsByTagName method

Similar to the `ID` method, `getElementsByTagName(<Name Of Tag>)` gets us elements with a couple of differences:

- It gives you a collection of elements instead of a single element (array)
- It queries for elements on the basis of their tag names and not `ID` values

Here's an example:

```
<div>My Content Here</div>
<script>
const div = document.getElementsByTagName('div')[0];
div.innerHTML = "Cool"; // above div's text is replaced with "Cool"
</script>
```

Notice the word `getElements`. It returns us a bunch of elements. Therefore, we pick up the first element from the `NodeList` and set its contents to `Cool`.

`innerHTML` is used to change the HTML content inside the element you're working on.

Using the getElementsByClassName method

The `getElementsByClassName` method will return elements of the same class as a `NodeList` and not an `Array`! `NodeList` is not exactly an `Array`; however, it is iterable, and easily convertible into `Array` as well:

```
<span class="tag">Hello</span>
<span class="tag">Hi</span>
```

```
<span class="tag">Wohoo!</span>

<script>
const tags = document.getElementsByClassName('tag'); // This is a NodeList
(not Array)
try {
  tags.map(tag => console.log(tag)); // ERROR! map is not a function
} catch(e) {
  console.log('Error ', e);
}

[...tags].map(tag => console.log(tag)); // No error
</script>
```

As said previously, `tags` is actually a `NodeList`. First, we use a destructuring operator and surround it with square brackets to actually convert it into an `Array`. Then we use `map` (which we can on `Array`, but cannot on `NodeList`) to iterate over every tag, that is, the `<span>` element, and we just console-log the element.

The takeaway from this code is how we used a destructuring operator in it. You'll often find yourself regularly using those important concepts we learned earlier.

Using the querySelector method

The `querySelector` method returns an element in the same way as when selecting an element through its CSS selector. However, `document.querySelector` returns only one element. Therefore, we can operate on it directly once we query for that element:

```
<div data-attr="coolDIV">Make me red!</div>
<script>
document.querySelector('div[data-attr]').style.color = 'red'; // div
becomes red
</script>
```

It is equivalent to doing `document.querySelector('div').style.color = 'red';` if we have only one `<div>` tag in the body.

Using the querySelectorAll method

Just like you can get any element with `querySelector`, you can get a bunch of elements matching the criteria with `querySelectorAll`. You've seen how to work with `NodeList` in the `getElementsByClass` method. Try to understand the code as follows:

```
<div data-attr="red">Make me red!</div>
<div data-attr="blue">Make me blue!</div>

<script>
[...document.querySelectorAll('div[data-attr]')].map(div => {
    div.style.color = div.attributes['data-attr'].value;
});
</script>
```

First, we're converting `NodeList` to `Array` using destructuring. Then we're mapping over the array and changing the style of each `<div>` according to the value of its data-attr.

Modern JavaScript browser APIs

HTML5 brought a lot of support for some awesome and cool APIs in JavaScript, right from the start. Although some APIs were released with HTML5 itself (such as the Canvas API), some were added later (such as the Fetch API).

Let's see some of these APIs and how to use them with some code examples.

Page Visibility API - is the user still on the page?

The **Page Visibility API** allows developers to run specific code whenever the page user is on goes in focus or out of foucs. Imagine you run a game-hosting site and want to pause the game whenever the user loses focus on your tab. This is the way to go!

```
function pageChanged() {
  if (document.hidden) {
    console.log('User is on some other tab/out of focus') // line #1
  } else {
    console.log('Hurray! User returned') // line #2
  }
}

document.addEventListener("visibilitychange", pageChanged);
```

We're adding an event listener to the document; it fires whenever the page is changed. Sure, the `pageChanged` function gets an event object as well in the argument, but we can simply use the `document.hidden` property, which returns a Boolean value depending on the page's visibility at the time the code was called.

You'll add your *pause game* code at `line #1` and your *resume game* code at `line #2`.

navigator.onLine API – the user's network status

The `navigator.onLine` API tells you if the user is online or not. Imagine building a multiplayer game and you want the game to automatically pause if the user loses their internet connection. This is the way to go here!

```
function state(e) {
    if(navigator.onLine) {
        console.log('Cool we\'re up');
    } else {
        console.log('Uh! we\'re down!');
    }
}

window.addEventListener('offline', state);
window.addEventListener('online', state);
```

Here, we're attaching two event listeners to window global. We want to call the `state` function whenever the user goes `offline` or `online`.

The browser will call the `state` function every time the user goes `offline` or `online`. We can access it if the user is `offline` or `online` with `navigator.onLine`, which returns a Boolean value of `true` if there's an internet connection, and `false` if there's not.

Clipboard API - programmatically manipulating the clipboard

The **Clipboard API** finally allows developers to copy to a user's clipboard without those nasty Adobe Flash plugin hacks that were not cross-browser/cross-device-friendly. Here's how you'll copy a selection to a user's clipboard:

```
<script>
function copy2Clipboard(text) {
  const textarea = document.createElement('textarea');
```

```
    textarea.value = text;
    document.body.appendChild(textarea);
    textarea.focus();
    textarea.setSelectionRange(0, text.length);
    document.execCommand('copy');
    document.body.removeChild(textarea);
  }
  </script>

  <button onclick="copy2Clipboard('Something good!')">Click me!</button>
```

First of all, we need the user to actually click the button. Once the user clicks the button, we call a function that creates a `textarea` in the background using the `document.createElement` method. The script then sets the value of the `textarea` to the passed text (this is pretty good!) We then focus on that `textarea` and select all the contents inside it.

Once the contents are selected, we execute a copy with `document.execCommand('copy')`; this copies the current selection in the document to the clipboard. Since, right now, the value inside the `textarea` is selected, it gets copied to the clipboard. Finally, we remove the `textarea` from the document so that it doesn't disrupt the document layout.

You cannot trigger `copy2Clipboard` without user interaction. I mean, obviously you can, but `document.execCommand('copy')` will not work if the event does not come from the user (click, double-click, and so on). This is a security implementation so that a user's clipboard is not messed around with by every website that they visit.

The Canvas API - the web's drawing board

HTML5 finally brought in support for `<canvas>`, a standard way to draw graphics on the web! Canvas can be used pretty much for everything related to graphics you can think of; from digitally signing with a pen, to creating 3D games on the web (3D games require WebGL knowledge, interested? - visit `http://bit.ly/webgl-101`).

Let's look at the basics of the Canvas API with a simple example:

```
<canvas id="canvas" width="100" height="100"></canvas>

<script>
  const canvas = document.getElementById("canvas");
  const ctx = canvas.getContext("2d");
  ctx.moveTo(0,0);
```

```
    ctx.lineTo(100, 100);
    ctx.stroke();
  </script>
```

This renders the following:

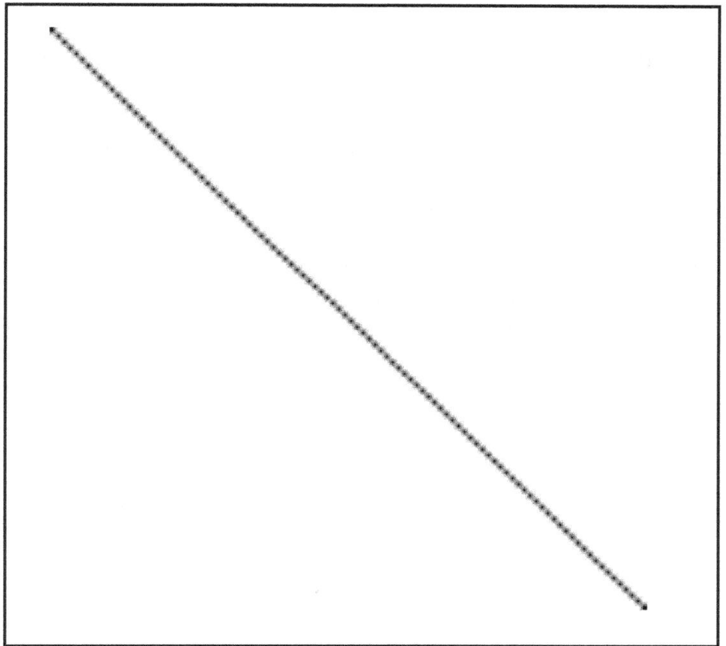

How does it do this?

1. Firstly, `document.getElementById('canvas')` gives us the reference to the canvas on the document.
2. Then we get the **context** of the canvas. This is a way to say what I want to do with the canvas. You could put a 3D value there, of course! That is indeed the case when you're doing 3D rendering with WebGL and canvas.
3. Once we have a reference to our context, we can do a bunch of things and add methods provided by the API out-of-the-box. Here we moved the cursor to the (0, 0) coordinates.
4. Then we drew a line till (100,100) (which is basically a diagonal on the square canvas).
5. Then we called stroke to actually draw that on our canvas. Easy!

Canvas is a wide topic and deserves a book of its own! If you're interested in developing awesome games and apps with Canvas, I recommend you start off with MDN docs: `http://bit.ly/canvas-html5`.

The Fetch API - promise-based HTTP requests

One of the coolest async APIs introduced in browsers is the Fetch API, which is the modern replacement for the `XMLHttpRequest` API. Have you ever found yourself using jQuery just for simplifying AJAX requests with $.ajax? If you have, then this is surely a golden API for you, as it is **natively** easier to code and read!

If you remember, we created a promised version of `XMLHttpRequest` ourselves in `Chapter 4`, *Asynchronous Programming*. However, `fetch` comes natively, hence, there are performance benefits. Let's see how it works:

```
fetch(link)
.then(data => {
    // do something with data
})
.catch(err => {
    // do something with error
});
```

Awesome! So `fetch` uses promises! If that's the case, we can combine it with async/await to make it look completely synchronous and easy to read!

```
<img id="img1" alt="Mozilla logo" />
<img id="img2" alt="Google logo" />

const get2Images = async () => {
    const image1 = await
fetch('https://cdn.mdn.mozilla.net/static/img/web-docs-sprite.22a6a085cf14.
svg');
    const image2 = await
fetch('https://www.google.com/images/branding/googlelogo/1x/googlelogo_colo
r_150x54dp.png');
    console.log(image1); // gives us response as an object
    const blob1 = await image1.blob();
    const blob2 = await image2.blob();
    const url1 = URL.createObjectURL(blob1);
    const url2 = URL.createObjectURL(blob2);

    document.getElementById('img1').src = url1;
```

```
        document.getElementById('img2').src = url2;

        return 'complete';
    }

    get2Images().then(status => console.log(status));
```

The line `console.log(image1)` will print the following:

```
▼ Response {type: "cors", url: "https://cdn.mdn.mozilla.net/static/img/web-docs-sprite.22a6a085cf14.svg", redirected:
  false, status: 200, ok: true, …}
  ▶ body: ReadableStream
    bodyUsed: true
  ▶ headers: Headers {}
    ok: true
    redirected: false
    status: 200
    statusText: ""
    type: "cors"
    url: "https://cdn.mdn.mozilla.net/static/img/web-docs-sprite.22a6a085cf14.svg"
  ▶ __proto__: Response
```

You can see the `image1` response provides tons of information about the request. It has an interesting field body, which is actually a `ReadableStream`, and a byte stream of data that can be cast to a **Binary Large Object** (**BLOB**) in our case.

A `blob` object represents a file-like object of immutable and raw data.

After getting the `Response`, we convert it into a `blob` object so that we can actually use it as an image. Here, fetch is actually fetching us the image directly so we can serve it to the user as a `blob` (without hot-linking it to the main website).

Thus, this could be done on the server side, and `blob` data could be passed down a WebSocket or something similar.

Fetch API customization

The Fetch API is highly customizable. You can even include your own headers in the request. Suppose you've got a site where only authenticated users with a valid token can access an image. Here's how you'll add a custom header to your request:

```
const headers = new Headers();
headers.append("Allow-Secret-Access", "yeah-because-my-token-is-1337");

const config = { method: 'POST', headers };

const req = new
Request('http://myawesomewebsite.awesometld/secretimage.jpg', config);

fetch(req)
.then(img => img.blob())
.then(blob => myImageTag.src = URL.createObjectURL(blob));
```

Here, we added a custom header to our `Request` and then created something called a `Request` object (an object that has information about our `Request`). The first parameter, that is, `http://myawesomewebsite.awesometld/secretimage.jpg`, is the URL and the second is the configuration. Here are some other configuration options:

- **Credentials**: Used to pass cookies in a **Cross-Origin Resource Sharing** (**CORS**)-enabled server on cross-domain requests.
- **Method**: Specifies request methods (GET, POST, HEAD, and so on).
- **Headers**: Headers associated with the request.
- **Integrity**: A security feature that consists of a (possibly) SHA-256 representation of the file you're requesting, in order to verify whether the request has been tampered with (data is modified) or not. Probably not a lot to worry about unless you're building something on a very large scale and not on HTTPS.
- **Redirect**: Redirect can have three values:
    - Follow: Will follow the URL redirects
    - Error: Will throw an error if the URL redirects
    - Manual: Doesn't follow redirect but returns a filtered response that wraps the redirect response
- **Referrer**: the URL that appears as a referrer header in the HTTP request.

Accessing and modifying history with the history API

You can access a user's history to some level and modify it according to your needs using the `history` API. It consists of the length and state properties:

```
console.log(history, history.length, history.state);
```

The output is as follows:

```
{length: 4, scrollRestoration: "auto", state: null}
4
null
```

In your case, the `length` could obviously be different depending on how many pages you've visited from that particular tab.

`history.state` can contain anything you like (we'll come to its use case soon). Before looking at some handy history methods, let us take a look at the `window.onpopstate` event.

Handling window.onpopstate events

The `window.onpopstate` event is fired automatically by the browser when a user navigates between history states that a developer has set. This event is important to handle when you push to history object and then later retrieve information whenever the user presses the **back/forward** button of the browser.

Here's how we'll program a simple `popstate` event:

```
window.addEventListener('popstate', e => {
    console.log(e.state); // state data of history (remember history.state
?)
})
```

Now we'll discuss some methods associated with the `history` object.

Modifying history - the history.go(distance) method

`history.go(x)` is equivalent to the user clicking his forward button `x` times in the browser. However, you can specify the distance to move, that is `history.go(5);` . This equivalent to the user hitting the **forward** button in the browser five times.

Similarly, you can specify negative values as well to make it move backward. Specifying 0 or no value will simply refresh the page:

```
history.go(5); // forwards the browser 5 times
history.go(-1); // similar effect of clicking back button
history.go(0); // refreshes page
history.go(); // refreshes page
```

Jumping ahead - the history.forward() method

This method is simply the equivalent of `history.go(1)`.

This is handy when you want to just push the user to the page he/she is coming from. One use case of this is when you can create a full-screen immersive web application and on your screen there are some minimal controls that play with the history behind the scenes:

```
if(awesomeButtonClicked && userWantsToMoveForward()) {
    history.forward()
}
```

Going back - the history.back() method

This method is simply the equivalent of `history.go(-1)`.

A negative number, makes the history go backwards. Again, this is just a simple (and numberless) way to go back to a page the user came from. Its application could be similar to a **forward** button, that is, creating a full-screen web app and providing the user with an interface to navigate by.

Pushing on the history - history.pushState()

This is really fun. You can change the browser URL without hitting the server with an HTTP request. If you run the following JS in your browser, your browser will change the path from whatever it is (`domain.com/abc/egh`) to `/i_am_awesome` (`domain.com/i_am_awesome`) without actually navigating to any page:

```
history.pushState({myName: "Mehul"}, "This is title of page",
"/i_am_awesome");
history.pushState({page2: "Packt"}, "This is page2", "/page2_packt"); // <-
- state is currently here
```

The History API doesn't care whether the page actually exists on the server or not. It'll just replace the URL as it is instructed.

The `popstate` event when triggered with the browser's back/forward button, will fire the function below and we can program it like this:

```
window.onpopstate = e => { // when this is called, state is already
updated.
    // e.state is the new state. It is null if it is the root state.
    if(e.state !== null) {
        console.log(e.state);
    } else {
        console.log("Root state");
    }
}
```

To run this code, run the `onpopstate` event first, then the two lines of `history.pushState` previously. Then press your browser's back button. You should see something like:

```
{myName: "Mehul"}
```

which is the information related to the parent state. Press back button one more time and you'll see the message `Root State`.

`pushState` does not fire `onpopstate` event. Only browsers' back/forward buttons do.

Pushing on the history stack - history.replaceState()

The `history.replaceState()` method is exactly like `history.pushState()`, the only difference is that it replaces the current page with another, that is, if you use `history.pushState()` and press the **back** button, you'll be directed to the page you came from.

However, when you use `history.replaceState()` and you press the **back** button, you are not directed to the page you came from because it is replaced with the new one on the stack. Here's an example of working with the `replaceState` method:

```
history.replaceState({myName: "Mehul"}, "This is title of page",
"/i_am_awesome");
```

This replaces (instead of pushing) the current state with the new state.

Although using the History API directly in your code may not be beneficial to you right now, many frameworks and libraries such as React, under the hood, use the History API to create a seamless, reload-less, smooth experience for the end user.

Summary

In this chapter, we covered some of the best APIs introduced by HTML5 and modern JavaScript together, and how they are shaping the way people browse and interact with websites.

In the next chapter, we'll take a brief overview of the HTTP protocol and some storage APIs available in JavaScript that can be used to store data locally and communicate with the server. Let's go!

10
Storage APIs in JavaScript

Imagine you're on Facebook and have logged in to your account. You see your news feed; everything looks normal. Next, you click on a post, and you're made to log in again. That's strange. You continue and log in one more time, and the post opens. You click on a link in a comment, and you're made to log in yet again. What is happening?

That's what would happen if we lived in a world without storage APIs on the frontend.

In this chapter, we'll take a look at the following topics:

- How the internet works because of cookies
- Different forms of data storage areas available in JavaScript
- Methods associated with `localStorage` and `sessionStorage` objects
- An introduction to `indexedDB`
- How to use `indexedDB` to perform basic adding, deleting, and reading operations

HyperText Transfer Protocol (HTTP)

HTTP is a stateless protocol. A stateless protocol means that there is no state being stored on the server, which, in turn, means that the server forgets everything once it has sent a response to the client. Consider the following situation:

You've typed `http://example.com` in your browser. When your request hits the server, the server is aware of your IP address, your requested page, and any other headers associated with your HTTP request. It fetches the content from the filesystem or database, sends the response to you, and then forgets about it.

Upon every new HTTP request, the client and server interact as if they're meeting for the first time. So, doesn't that mean our earlier Facebook example is true in the real world as well?

Essentially, that is the case. All websites use **cookies** for authentication purposes, which is a way to fake the statefulness of a protocol. Remove cookies from every request and you will be able to see the raw, stateless HTTP protocol in front of you.

What is a TLS/SSL handshake?

Let's take a minute to understand what the **Transport Layer Security** (**TLS**)/**Secure Sockets Layer** (**SSL**) is before actually diving into what the heck a handshake is.

First of all, we should note that TLS is just an upgraded, and more modern, version of SSL. So, what's SSL?

SSL is a standard within security protocols for setting up an encrypted and secure tunnel between your computer and the remote server. It prevents somebody who is eavesdropping on your internet connection, say your **Internet Service Provider** (**ISP**), from stealing data that is transferred over the network.

On every major site these days, you will see a green lock to the left of the URL inside the browser. That is a symbol of security, and it means that your browser is using TLS/SSL encryption to communicate with the server.

Now, what is a handshake? Just like the literal meaning, a handshake is where your browser and server exchange the cryptographic keys they'll use in each communication to encrypt or decrypt the messages sent by one another.

Why are we discussing TLS/SSL? It is because TLS/SSL handshakes are expensive on performance. They are not really expensive when there is just one handshake, but they start to become a problem if we introduce the concept of statelessness. This means that your browser and server forget that they already know each other's cryptographic keys with every request. This means that your browser and server need to perform a TLS handshake with every request, which will make everything quite slow. To avoid this, the TLS/SSL protocol is actually a stateful protocol.

The reason why HTTP is so scalable is that it is stateless. Stateful protocols such as TLS and SSL are heavy to implement logically. If you want to know more about how TLS/SSL works, read here: https://security.stackexchange.com/a/20833/44281

Mimicking an HTTP state

Using a cookie is a way to store a small amount of data related to a user visiting your site. You'll learn more about cookies in the next section. Whatever you store in cookies on a particular website is attached to every HTTP request to that site. So, basically, your HTTP protocol transfers a string of cookies on every request that allows the server to store some sort of information related to each client connected to it.

When we add custom headers to our `XMLHttpRequest` (remember T*he Fetch API customizations* section from the preceding chapter?), it makes it easy to fake our own state on the HTTP protocol. An authorization header is one more header that is sent by the browser on every request if it is set.

Let's now actually take a look at these storage areas, such as cookies, `localStorage`, `sessionStorage`, and `indexedDB`.

Storing data with cookies

Cookies are little strings, which, once set for a domain and path, are sent over and over to the server for every request. This is perfect for authentication, but not so good if you're using them to store some data that you need only once or that you need to access only on the frontend, such as a player's score in a game whose results you are not storing on the server.

People usually use cookies to store heavy data to make it available on some other path on the domain. This is a bad practice because you're transferring that data to the server all the time, and, if that data is heavy, it'll make your communication slow.

Setting cookies

Let's take a look at how to access and set cookies using JavaScript:

Information found within a cookie is in the `key=value;` format. Let us create some cookies in the browser using the code snippet below:

```
document.cookie = "myFirstCookie=good;"
document.cookie = "mySecondCookie=great;"
console.log(document.cookie);
```

Warning: Strange behavior ahead!

What do you expect to be logged here? The answer is as follows:

```
document.cookie = "myFirstCookie=good;"
document.cookie = "mySecondCookie=great;"
console.log(document.cookie);
myFirstCookie=good; mySecondCookie=great
```

Why, and why wasn't the `document.cookie` object overwritten? All will be explained in the next section.

The document.cookie is a strange object

As you saw earlier, `document.cookie` shows a special behavior. Instead of replacing all cookies, it updates the variable to the new cookie. This behavior is implemented by a document that is actually called a **host object** instead of a native object. Host objects have the power to do anything, as they don't need to follow the semantics for regular objects.

Host objects are actually the objects provided in a particular environment--in our case, the browser. When JavaScript runs on the server (Node.js), you do not have access to a document or window. That means they're host objects--that is, dependent on hosts and implemented by hosts (browsers).

In this case, `document.cookie` overrides the assignment operator to actually append the value to the variable instead of modifying it.

More technical information about `[[PutValue]]` from the specs can be found at `http://es5.github.io/#x8.7.2`.

The question is now how do we remove the cookies we set? We'll take a look in the next section.

Deleting cookies

To delete a cookie, you return to the cookie and then specify an expiry date for it. After which, the browser will delete the cookie and no longer send it to the server on every request.

Here's how to implement that in code:

```
document.cookie = "myFirstCookie=good;"
document.cookie = "mySecondCookie=great;"
console.log(document.cookie);
document.cookie = "mySecondCookie=; expires=Thu, 01 Jan 1970 00:00:00 GMT";
console.log(document.cookie);
```

`1 January 1970 00:00:00` is as far back in time as we can go, as JavaScript follows Unix's timestamp. The output for the preceding code is as follows:

```
document.cookie = "myFirstCookie=good;"
document.cookie = "mySecondCookie=great;"
console.log(document.cookie);
document.cookie = "mySecondCookie=; expires=Thu, 01 Jan 1970 00:00:00 GMT";
console.log(document.cookie);
myFirstCookie=good; mySecondCookie=great
myFirstCookie=good
```

Getting a cookie value

JavaScript doesn't provide any convenient way out of the box to actually get a cookie value. All we have is just a bunch of random cookies together in a string, which is accessible by `document.cookie`. We will need to do some work, as shown in the following snippet:

```
document.cookie = "awesomecookie=yes;";
document.cookie = "ilovecookies=sure;";
document.cookie = "great=yes";

function getCookie(name) {
    const cookies = document.cookie.split(';');
    for(let i=0;i < cookies.length;i++) {
        if(cookies[i].trim().indexOf(name) === 0) {
            return cookies[i].split('=')[1];
        }
    }
    return null;
}
```

```
console.log(getCookie("ilovecookies"));
console.log(getCookie("doesnotexist"));
```

The output will be, therefore, as follows:

```
sure
null
```

As you can see in the highlighted part of the image below, when we reload the page, the set cookies are sent to the server at every request:

```
▼ Request Headers      view parsed
   GET / HTTP/1.1
   Host: localhost:3000
   Connection: keep-alive
   Cache-Control: max-age=0
   Upgrade-Insecure-Requests: 1
   User-Agent: Mozilla/5.0 (Macintosh; Intel Mac OS X 10_13
   like Gecko) Chrome/63.0.3239.132 Safari/537.36
   Accept: text/html,application/xhtml+xml,application/xml;
   *;q=0.8
   Accept-Encoding: gzip, deflate, br
   Accept-Language: en-US,en;q=0.9,fr;q=0.8,sr;q=0.7
   Cookie: awesomecookie=yes; ilovecookies=sure; great=yes
```

These will later become accessible by the server, depending on the backend language you're using.

Working with localStorage

The `localStorage` object is available in all major browsers. It was introduced in HTML5. Local storage allows you to store data persistently on a user's computer. Unless your script or user explicitly want to clear the data, the data will remain.

Local storage follows the same origin policy. We will discuss origin policy in detail in the next chapter, but, for now, just understand that the same origin policies can restrict different websites and their access to a particular website's local storage.

In addition, keep in mind that key-value pairs in local storage can only be string values. To store objects, you'll have to `JSON.stringify` them first.

Creating a local storage entry

We can add entries to local storage in a more intuitive and convenient way than cookies. Here's what the syntax looks like using `localStorage.setItem(key, value)`:

```
localStorage.setItem('myKey', 'awesome value');
console.log('entry added');
```

The `localStorage` is a synchronous API. It'll block the thread execution until completed.

Let's now quickly, and roughly, determine how much time on average `localStorage.setItem` takes, as follows:

```
const now = performance.now();

for(let i=0;i<1000;i++) {
    localStorage.setItem(`myKey${i}`, `myValue${i}`);
}

const then = performance.now();
console.log('Done')
console.log(`Time taken: ${(then - now)/1000} milliseconds per operation`);
```

The result, as you can see, is not that bad:

```
Done
Time taken: 0.020700000000942964 milliseconds per operation
```

So, it roughly takes around `0.02` milliseconds for one operation. That's good going for a regular application.

Getting a stored item

A stored item inside a session storage object can be accessed using the `localStorage.getItem`, `localStorage.key`, or `localStorage['key']` methods. We'll take a look at this in more detail a little later, in the `localStorage.getItem('key')` versus `localStorage.key` section, where we'll see which method is the best and why not to use other methods; now, though, let's stick with the `localStorage.getItem` method.

It's easy to get stored items from local storage, as shown in the following snippet:

```
const item = localStorage.getItem('myKey');
console.log(item); // my awesome value
```

Removing a stored item

You can remove a single item from the `localStorage` object. For this, you will need to have the key of the key-value pair you want to remove. This could be anything you no longer need.

Accessing it further in your code will result in `null`, as follows:

```
localStorage.removeItem('myKey');
console.log(localStorage.getItem('myKey')); // null
```

Clearing all the items

Sometimes, you might find while experimenting that you've put a lot of useless key-value pairs inside your storage. You can clear them all at once with the `clear` method in local storage. You can do that with the following command:

```
localStorage.clear();
console.log(localStorage); // blank object {}
```

localStorage.getItem('key') versus localStorage.key versus localStorage['key']

All three, `localStorage.getItem('key')`, `localStorage.key`, and `localStorage['key']` methods, do the same thing. However, it is advisable to use the provided methods for the following reasons:

- `localStorage.getItem('key-does-not-exist')` returns `null`, whereas `localStorage['key-does-not-exist']` will return `undefined`. In JavaScript, `null` is not equal to `undefined`. For example, suppose that you want to set a key that is actually the property of an object as well, or as a function name, such as `getItem` and `setItem`. In this case, you're better off with the `getItem` approach, as follows:

  - ```
    localStorage.setItem('getItem', 'whohoo we are not overwriting getItem'); // #1
    localStorage.getItem('getItem'); // whohoo we are not overwriting getItem

    localStorage.getItem = 'oh no I'm screwed'; // #2
    localStorage.getItem('getItem'); // Error! getItem is not a function.
    ```

- If you accidentally used the notation `#2` instead of `#1` to store a number, `localStorage` will overwrite the `getItem` function, and you will no longer be able to access it, as shown in the following snippet:

  - ```
    localStorage.setItem('length', 100); // Stores "1" as string in localStorage
    localStorage.length = 100; // Ignored by localStorage
    ```

The takeaway here is to use the `getItem`, `setItem`, and other methods on `localStorage`.

Working with SessionStorage

Session storage is just like local storage, with the exception that session storage is not persistent. That means whenever you close even the tab that sets the session storage, your data will be lost.

A case where session storage could be useful could be when you have an Ajax-based website that loads everything dynamically. You want to create a state-like object, which you can use to store the state of the interface so that, when a user returns to a page they have already visited, you can easily restore the state of that page.

Let's now quickly go over all the methods of session storage.

Creating a session storage entry

To create a key-value pair inside the `sessionStorage` object, you can use the `setItem` method, similar to the `localStorage` object. Just like `localStorage`, `sessionStorage` is also a synchronous API, so you can be sure that you'll immediately have access to whatever values you're storing.

Adding an item to session storage is just like working with local storage, as shown in the following snippet:

```
sessionStorage.setItem('my key', 'awesome value');
console.log('Added to session storage');
```

Getting a stored item

A stored item inside the `sessionStorage` object can be accessed using the `sessionStorage.getItem`, `sessionStorage.key`, or `sessionStorage['key']` methods. However, as with `localStorage`, it is advisable to make use of `getItem` to safely get the right storage value instead of a property of the `sessionStorage` object.

The following snippet demonstrates how to get a stored item from session storage:

```
const item = sessionStorage.getItem('myKey');
console.log(item); // my awesome value
```

Removing a stored item

You can remove a single item from the `sessionStorage` object. For this, you will need to have the key of the key-value pair you want to remove. This could be anything you no longer need.

Accessing it further in your code will result in `null`, as shown in the following snippet:

```
sessionStorage.removeItem('myKey');
console.log(sessionStorage.getItem('myKey')); // null
```

Clearing all items

Sometimes, you might find while experimenting that you've put a lot of useless key-value pairs inside your storage. You can clear them all at once with the `clear` method in session storage, as shown in the following snippet:

```
sessionStorage.clear();
console.log(sessionStorage); // blank object {}
```

Handling storage changes across multiple tabs

Storage, when changed, emits certain events that can be captured by other opened tabs. You can set event listeners for them to listen and perform any appropriate modifications.

For example, let's say that you added something to `localStorage` in one tab of your website. A user has also opened another tab of your website. If you want to reflect the changes of `localStorage` in that tab, you can listen to the storage event and update the contents accordingly.

Note that the update event will be fired on every other tab except the one that made the change:

```
window.addEventListener('storage', e => {
  console.log(e);
});
localStorage.setItem('myKey', 'myValue'); // note that this line was run in
another tab
```

The preceding code produces the following output:

```
▼ StorageEvent {isTrusted: true, key: "myKey", oldValue: "myValue2", newValue: "myValue23", url: "https://developer.mozilla.org/en-US/docs/Web/API/Web_Storage_API/Using_the_Web_Storage_API", …}
    bubbles: false
    cancelBubble: false
    cancelable: false
    composed: false
  ► currentTarget: Window {postMessage: ƒ, blur: ƒ, focus: ƒ, close: ƒ, frames: Window, …}
    defaultPrevented: false
    eventPhase: 2
    isTrusted: true
    key: "myKey"
    newValue: "myValue23"
    oldValue: "myValue2"
  ► path: [Window]
    returnValue: true
  ► srcElement: Window {postMessage: ƒ, blur: ƒ, focus: ƒ, close: ƒ, frames: Window, …}
  ► storageArea: Storage {myKey: "myValue23", taskTracker: "1518882922193", length: 2}
  ► target: Window {postMessage: ƒ, blur: ƒ, focus: ƒ, close: ƒ, frames: Window, …}
    timeStamp: 1286384.965
    type: "storage"
    url: "https://developer.mozilla.org/en-US/docs/Web/API/Web_Storage_API/Using_the_Web_Storage_API"
  ► __proto__: StorageEvent
```

You can note that it contains a lot of useful information about the storage event.

The web workers (discussed in Chapter 11) do not have access to local storage or session storage.

Cookies versus local storage

By now, you may have observed that cookies and local storage serve almost completely different purposes. The only thing they have in common is that they store data. The following is a brief comparison of cookies and local storage:

Cookies	**Local storage**
Cookies are transferred to a server on every request automatically by the browser	To transfer local storage data to a server, you need to manually send an Ajax request or send it through hidden form fields
If data needs to be accessed and read both by the client and server, use cookies	If the data needs to be accessed and read only by the client, use local storage

Cookies can have an expiration date, after which they are automatically deleted	Local storage provides no such expiration date feature; it can only be cleared by JavaScript
The maximum size of a cookie is 4 KB	The maximum size of local storage depends on the browser and platform, but it is usually around 5 MB per domain

The indexedDB - storing large data

The `indexedDB` is a relatively new and low-level API compared to the other storage mediums we've already discussed. It is used to store large amounts of data compared to local storage. However, the drawback of this is that it is difficult to be used and set up.

What you can do with local storage in a few lines may take a lot of lines and callbacks in `indexedDB`. Therefore, be careful when using it. If you're using it in your application, we recommend that you use popular wrappers instead of directly writing the endpoints, as that will make things easier.

The `indexedDB` is so vast that it would be fair to say it deserves a whole chapter on its own. We can't cover each and every aspect in this chapter, but we'll try to convey the key information required.

Opening an indexedDB database

The `indexedDB` object is available on the `window` object. You will need to actually open a database in order to store data in `indexedDB`, shown as follows:

```
const open = window.indexedDB.open("myDB", 1);
```

You have to first request to open the database from `indexedDB`. The first parameter here is the name of your database. If it doesn't exist, it'll be created automatically.

The second parameter is the version number of the database. What that means is that you can assign a version number to every database schema, which is useful in the following example.

Consider that you shipped your application that is using `indexedDB`. Now, `indexedDB` consists of a database schema, which lays down certain rules on how the data should look in the database, its data types, and so on. However, you soon realize that you need to update your database design. Now, you can ship your production code with `indexedDB.open`, but with a higher version. This further enables you to know within your code that your older database schema may be incompatible with the new one.

If the database already existed and you opened it with a higher version number (say 2, in our case), then it'll fire the `upgradeneeded` event, which you can handle in the code.

Version numbers only supports integers. Any floating number passed will be rounded off to the closest lower integer. For example, passing 2.3 as a version number is the same as passing 2.

Handling the upgradeneeded event

As discussed previously, we can now handle the `upgradeneeded` event. As we have just created the database for the first time, the following `upgradeneeded` event will be fired:

```
const open = window.indexedDB.open("types", 1);

// Let us create a schema for the database
open.onupgradeneeded = () => {
    const dbHandler = open.result;
    const storeHandler = dbHandler.createObjectStore("frontend");
};
```

Okay, in the preceding code, we got the `IDBDatabase` object handler, which we call `dbHandler`, by calling `open.result`.

Then, we created something called an object store in `indexedDB`. Object stores are like tables in `indexedDB`, where the data is stored in the form of key-value pairs.

Adding data to object stores

We can use `storeHandler` to actually put data inside a table with the following code:

```
const open = window.indexedDB.open("types", 1);

open.onupgradeneeded = () => {
    const dbHandler = open.result;
    const storeHandler = dbHandler.createObjectStore("frontend");
    storeHandler.add({
        latestVersion: 5,
        cool: "yes",
        easy2use: "yes"
    }, "HTML5");
};
```

Let's take a moment to understand what just happened. By calling `storeHandler.add()`, we were able to add data to our `frontend` table inside our `types` database (version 1). The first argument--that is, our passed object--is the value, which can be an object in `indexedDB`. Values can only be strings in `localStorage`. The second argument--that is, `HTML5`--is the name of our key.

The result should look like the following screenshot:

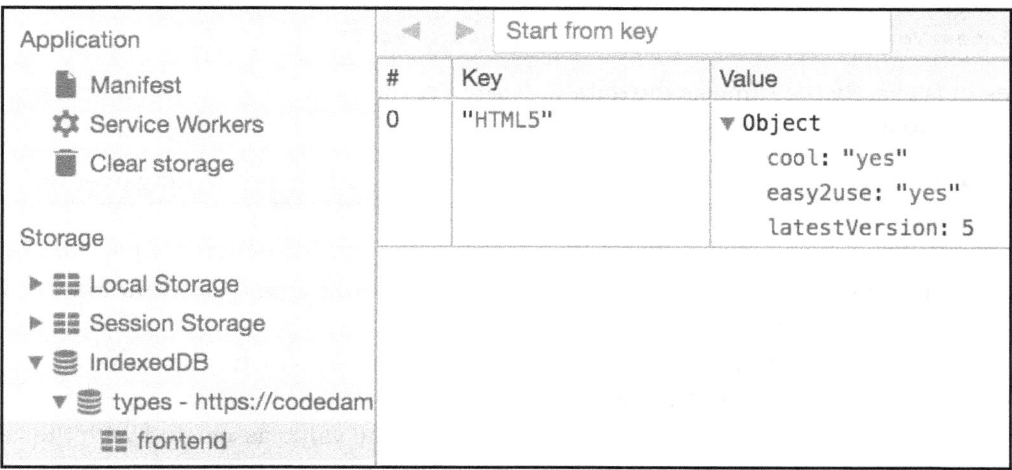

In the preceding screenshot, you should be able to see the `indexedDB`, `types` database, and then a table called `frontend` that stores the key as `HTML5` and the value as our supplied object.

Reading data from object stores

Whenever a connection is established, the `onsuccess` event is fired. Only read-write operations in the `onupgradeneeded` work because it won't be fired if the version number of the database is not increased.

As a matter of fact, we recommend changing the database schema from the `onupgradeneeded` event. When you're in `onsuccess`, perform only the CRUD operations (which are Create, Update, Retrieve, and Delete).

We can do our operations inside the `success` event with the following code:

```
const open = window.indexedDB.open("types", 1); // same database as above
open.onsuccess = () => {
    const dbHandler = open.result;
    const transaction = dbHandler.transaction(['frontend'], 'readonly');
    const storeHandler = transaction.objectStore('frontend');
    const req = storeHandler.get("HTML5");
    req.onsuccess = e => {
        console.log(e.target.result);
    }
};
```

The output of the program is as follows:

```
{latestVersion: 5, cool: "yes", easy2use: "yes"}
```

The result is exactly the same as the data we stored earlier, but what are the transactions? They are as follows:

- The `indexedDB` uses transactions to perform reading and writing over the database
- We first open a transaction to our database `frontend` in the `readonly` mode; the other mode is the `readwrite` mode, which is used when you want to write to the database as well
- From that transaction, we then get `storeHandler`, which is the same as the store handler we had in an earlier section when we created the store
- Now, we make use of the `get` method to get the value associated with the key we stored
- We then wait for `req` to call the `success` event, on which we console log the target result value, which is nothing but our stored object

Deleting data from object stores

Similar to writing and reading, we can also delete data from the object store, as well, as follows:

```
const open = window.indexedDB.open("types", 1); // same database as above
open.onsuccess = () => {
    const dbHandler = open.result;
    const transaction = dbHandler.transaction(['frontend'], 'readwrite');
    const storeHandler = transaction.objectStore('frontend');
    storeHandler.delete("HTML5");
};
```

The only thing we did here was using the `delete` method. Note that we have to give the `readwrite` access to the transaction in order to delete the record.

It's recommended that you go through MDN documents to get a deeper insight on how to make `indexedDB` work in big projects; you can find them at `https://developer.mozilla.org/en-US/docs/Web/API/IndexedDB_API/Using_IndexedDB`.

Summary

Great! That's one more concept we've now equipped ourselves with. In this chapter, you learned how to store data on the client side effectively, and how cookies are sent automatically to the server by browsers. In the next two chapters, we will dive deep into web workers and shared memory, which can create some very powerful stuff when combined together. Let's go!

11
Web and Service Workers

Let's suppose that you are building a cool web app, say, to factorize a number to two prime numbers. Now, this involves a lot of CPU-intensive work, which will block the main UI thread. The main UI thread is the traffic lane that the end user directly observes and perceives. If it seems congested (laggy) or blocked, even for a few seconds, it destroys the user experience.

This is where web workers come into the picture. Web workers can be thought of as those side-lanes available on the road where you can divert heavy and slow (CPU-intensive) trucks so that you don't block a user's shining Lamborghini on the main road (the main UI thread).

On the other hand, service workers are quite cool, too. A service worker is your own programmable network proxy, which sits right in between the user's internet connection and your website. There will be more on that in the *Working with service workers* section.

In this chapter, we'll cover:

- Introduction to threads
- Introduction to web workers
- Introduction to dedicated workers
- Setting up dedicated workers
- Introduction to shared workers
- Setting up shared workers
- Setting up inline web workers
- Communication with the main thread
- Introduction to service workers
- Setting up service workers

An introduction to the concept of threads

Simply put, a thread is a simple and independent snippet of running code. It is a container in which your tasks get executed. Before web workers, JavaScript provided just a single thread; that is, the main thread for the developers to do everything in.

This created some problems with advancements in tech. Suppose you're running a smooth CSS3 animation, and suddenly you need to do a heavy calculation on the JavaScript end for some reason. This'll make the animation sluggish if you do it on the main thread. However, if you offload it to a web worker that runs in its own thread, it will have no effect on the user experience.

Because web workers run in their own threads, they cannot have access to the following:

- `DOM`: It is not thread-safe to access it from web workers and the main UI script
- `parent` object: Basically, this gives access to some DOM APIs that for the same reason as stated above, would be thread-unsafe to access
- `window` object: BOM (Browser Object Model); access to this is also thread-unsafe
- `document` object: `DOM` object; hence, thread-unsafe

Web workers lack access to all of the aforementioned items because it is not thread-safe to give workers access to them. Let's learn more about what I mean by that.

What makes something thread-safe?

When two or more threads access a common data source, extreme care must be taken, because there is a high chance of data corruption and thread safety conditions such as deadlocks, preconditions, race conditions, and so on.

JavaScript did not add thread support from the very start. With web workers introducing a **sort-of** threading environment in JavaScript, it'll help to understand a few conditions associated with threads in general.

What, exactly, is a deadlock?

A deadlock is a situation where two threads are waiting for each other, for whatever reasons, and the reasons of both threads depend on each other. The following figure will explain what deadlock means:

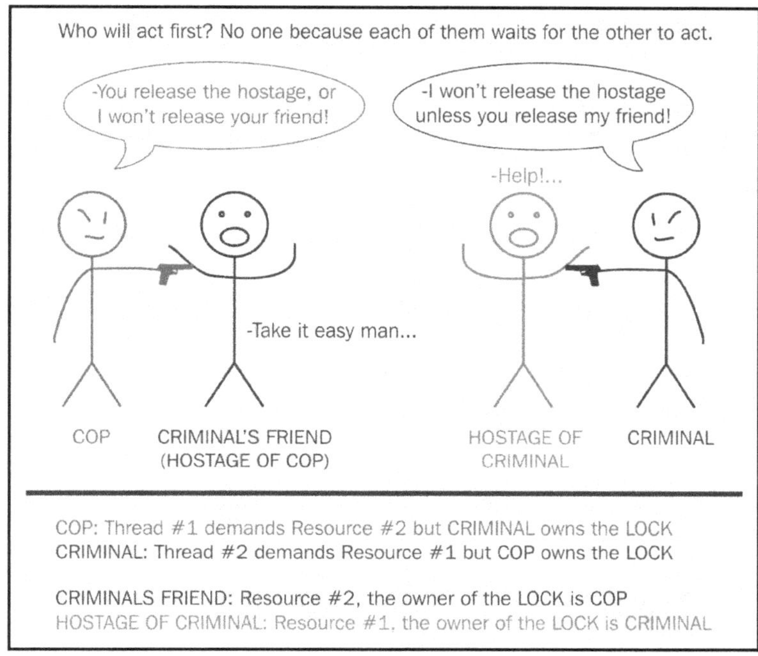

Clearly, both threads (people with guns) need the other thread's resource in order to proceed. So, nobody proceeds.

What, exactly, is a race condition?

A **race condition** is a problem that can happen if a DOM is allowed to be accessed by web workers. A race condition is a condition where two threads race, or compete, to read/modify a single data source. This is dangerous because when both threads try to modify the data at same time, and it is unknown which one will modify the data first. Consider the following example.

Suppose two threads are working on the same variable in memory:

```
// thread 1 - pseudo program code
if variable == 5:
    asyncOperationWhichTakes200MS()
    // just here thread 2 modifies variable to 10
    res = variable * 5
    // res is now 50 instead of 25
    // unpredicatable behavior ahead
```

Race conditions can be avoided by using **semaphores**, which is nothing but locking a shared data resource, until one thread is done with it and releases it back.

Just a fun fact: If you ever use `sudo apt-get update` on Ubuntu or any Linux distro supporting `apt-get` as the package manager, and try to run another `apt-get update` command in another Terminal, you'll get this error:

```
E: Unable to lock the administration directory
(/var/lib/dpkg/) is another process using it?
```

Linux locks the directory to avoid a possible race condition in which two commands overwrite each other's results.

Most languages have just a single thread that interacts with and updates the UI, and other threads can only post messages to the main thread to update the UI.

Introduction to web workers

The web worker is, essentially, a piece of JS code which does not run in the same thread as your main application. And by thread, I literally mean a different thread. The web workers truly enable JS to work in a multi-threaded mode. A question that might arise here is, What are the differences between asynchronous operations and web workers?

If you think about it, they are more or less the same thing. The web workers take away loads from the main thread for a while and then come back with the results. However understand the fact that `async` functions run on the UI thread, whereas web workers do not. Also, web workers are long-lived, and live inside a separate thread, whereas asynchronous operators, as we discussed in *Chapter 4, Asynchronous Programming,* follow the *Event loop*.

Performance-wise, web workers are also much faster than traditional asynchronous operations. Here's a test which sorts randomly generated arrays of lengths **10K** and **1M** as an asynchronous operation and web worker:

Testing in Chrome 63.0.3239 / Mac OS X 10.13.2		
	Test	Ops/sec
Sort 10k using web worker	`inlineWorker.postMessage(arr10k);`	2,493 ±33.46% fastest
Sort 10k using asynchronous JS	`jsNativeSort(arr10k);`	66.82 ±80.06% 98% slower
Sort 1M using web worker	`inlineWorker.postMessage(arr1mm);`	16.91 ±31.12% 99% slower
Sort 1M using asynchronous JS	`jsNativeSort(arr1mm);`	2.91 ±28.88% 100% slower

Take note that **2,493 ops/sec** means that JS was able to sort **2,493** arrays of length **10K** in **1** second! Async JS, on the other hand, was able to sort about 67 arrays of length **10K** in **1** second, which is still pretty darn fast, but quite a lot slower than its competitor.

Checking if worker support is available

Although web workers have been around for quite a long time and support is very strong, you still might want to check if web worker support is available in a client's browser (for example, Opera Mini doesn't support it). If it isn't, then just load the web worker file in the main script as well, and let your user feel the heat.

Web workers are available as a `window` object, so that is pretty much all you have to check in order to get started:

```
if(typeof window.Worker !== "function") {
    // worker not available
} else {
    // good to go
}
```

Working with dedicated web workers

Dedicated workers are the workers dedicated to a single main script. That means the worker cannot interact with any other script, apart from the main script on the page or any other domain.

Let us try to understand dedicated workers by setting one up.

Setting up a dedicated worker

Calling a `new Worker()` with a filename in the constructor argument is all you need to do to spawn a dedicated worker:

```
// script.js loaded on index.html

const awesomeWorker = new Worker('myworker.js');
```

Using the `new Worker` constructor, we created a `Worker` instance. This will make the browser download the `myworker.js` file and start a new OS thread for it.

This is what we can place in the `myworker.js` file:

```
// myworker.js
console.log('Hello world!');
```

This logs `Hello world` inside the console.

A worker can create a sub-worker itself, and everything below will apply to that, as well.

Working with dedicated workers

Dedicated workers can communicate with their spawning script, listening to certain events which trigger when either of the scripts sends/receives a message.

These events can be handled in both scripts (worker and main script) using certain event handlers. Let us learn how to achieve that.

Listening for messages on the main script

We can listen to what a worker sent to the main script with the `onmessage` event. This is how it'll look:

```
// script.js

const awesomeworker = new Worker('myworker.js');
awesomeworker.addEventListener('message', e => {
    console.log(e.data); // data sent by worker
});
```

Here, our script is listening for messages sent by the worker. Every time a worker sends a message (which we'll see how to do in a minute, in the *Sending messages from the main script* section), the previous event is triggered and we console the data.

Listening for messages on the worker script

Workers themselves have access to the `self` object, to which you can attach similar event listeners, as previously discussed. Let us see how that goes:

```
// myworker.js

self.addEventListener('message', e => {
    console.log(e.data); // data sent by main script
});
```

Here, the message event listener is fired whenever the main script sends a message to this particular web worker. We simply console-log what the main script sent with `console.log(e.data)`.

You can omit the `self` keyword here if you wish. By default, in workers, events will be attached to `self`.

Sending messages from the main script

Okay! Once you've set up the listener event correctly, you will want to send some tasks to the worker for it to do. This is how to achieve that:

```
// script.js

const awesomeworker = new Worker('myworker.js');
awesomeworker.addEventListener('message', e => {
    console.log(e.data); // data sent by worker
});

const data = {task: "add", nums: [5, 10, 15, 20]};

// lets send this data
awesomeworker.postMessage(data);
```

Alright. Here, we're giving a task to the worker to add two numbers. Note that we are able to pass objects/arrays to the `postMessage` method, which is actually used to post/deliver a message to the worker which is spawned.

Objects messaged through `postMessage` are copied and not referenced. This means that, if the worker script modifies this object in any way, it will not reflect in the main `script` object. This is important for message passing consistency.

Now we can receive this object at the other end (that is, the worker) and process it in the following way:

```
// myworker.js

self.addEventListener('message', e => {
    if(e.data.task == "add") {
        const res = e.data.nums.reduce((sum, num) => sum+num, 0);
        // do something with res
    }
});
```

Here, on receiving the message, we check if the main script wants the worker to add numbers. If that's the case, we reduce the array value to a single value using the inbuilt `reduce` method to add all numbers in the passed array.

Sending messages from the worker script

Similar to the main script, `postMessage` is used in the worker script to communicate to the main script. Let us see how to post the previous result to the main script:

```
// myworker.js

addEventListener('message', e => {
    if(e.data.task == "add") {
        const res = e.data.nums.reduce((sum, num) => sum+num, 0);
        postMessage({task: "add", result: res}); // self.postMessage will
also work
    }
});
```

Here, just like in the preceding code, we're reducing the array value to the `sum`, and then actually sending back whatever we did to the main UI script with the `postMessage` function. The passed object can be received by calling the script inside its own listening method.

`script.js` would look like the following:

```
// script.js

const awesomeworker = new Worker('myworker.js');
awesomeworker.addEventListener('message', e => {
    if(e.data.task == "add") {
    // task completed. do something with result
        document.write(e.data.result);
    }
});

const data = {task: "add", nums: [5, 10, 15, 20, 25, 30, 35, 40, 45, 50]};
awesomeworker.postMessage(data);
```

Here, you can see that we're sending the `task` to the worker in the form of an object, and the worker nicely performs the calculation and sends it to the main script, which is further handled by the message event listener attached to the `awesomeworker`, which simply writes the result to the document.

Error handling in workers

It is possible that your worker might throw an error because of malformed data sent by the main script. In that case, the `onerror` method of the worker is called in the main script:

```
// script.js

const awesomeworker = new Worker('myworker.js');
awesomeworker.postMessage({task: "divide", num1: 5, num2: 0})

awesomeworker.addEventListener('error', e => {
    console.log(e); // information of ErrorEvent
});
```

Here, we attached an error event listener, and for now, we're just logging it to the console. You might want to send it to a server to actually log it for further analysis in a production app.

The worker is as follows:

```
// myworker.js

self.addEventListener('message', e => {
    if(e.data.num2 == 0) {
        throw "Cannot divide by 0";
    } else {
        postMessage({task: "divide", result: e.data.num1/e.data.num2 });
    }
});
```

In the previous case, the worker throws an error, which is visible in the main script as an `ErrorEvent` object. From there, you can handle the error.

Throwing an error from a web worker doesn't permanently stop it from working. It is still usable unless terminated.

Terminating workers

You can terminate a worker when you think it is no longer required. You can terminate a worker from either the worker itself or the parent script. Let us see how to do this in the next section.

Terminating from the worker script

Sometimes, it might be required to terminate a worker within the worker when the worker is performing some sort of async task whose duration can be variable. There is a method called `close()` available inside the worker for that purpose:

```
// myworker.js

addEventListener('message', e => {
    if(e.data.message == "doAjaxAndDie") {
        fetch(...).then(data => {
            postMessage(data);
            close(); // or self.close();
        });
    }
});
```

Terminating from the main script

Similarly, you can terminate a worker from the main script, as well, if you wish to. After terminating, your worker instance can no longer be used to post messages to. It also kills any executing process in your worker:

```
// script.js

const awesomeworker = new Worker('myworker.js');

awesomeworker.addEventListener('message', e => {
    if(e.data.message == "killme") {
        awesomeworker.terminate(); // bye bye
        console.log("Worker terminated");
    }
});
```

The `myworker.js` file for this would be:

```
// myworker.js
// .. some work
postMessage({message: "killme"});
```

Killing from within the worker involves calling `close()`, while from the parent script it involves calling `terminate()` methods.

Transferring (not copying) data through postMessage

It is possible to actually just transfer large amounts of data using the `postMessage` function. What does that mean, and how it is different from what we've been doing so far with `postMessage`?

Well, the actual syntax of `postMessage` is: `postMessage(aMessage, transferList).`

What this means is, whatever you pass as `transferList` is apparently lost in the worker that sent it. You actually gave the other script the authority to own that data. You transferred the ownership of that data to that other script. Remember, this is different from what used to usually happen (that is, you can still access the object in the same script that sent it to the web worker/main script) because in this case, the data is not copied. Its ownership is transferred.

This makes it lightning fast to transfer very large amounts of data across web workers. Transferable objects include things like `ArrayBuffer`. Here's an example of how to work with it:

```
const ab = new ArrayBuffer(100);

// add data to this arraybuffer
console.log(ab.byteLength); // 100
worker.postMessage(ab, [ab]);
console.log(ab.byteLength); // 0 - ownership lost
```

You can see that the size of our `ArrayBuffer` went from 100 to 0. This is because you no longer have access to the `ArrayBuffer` memory, because you transferred it to some other script.

Working with shared workers

As discussed previously, shared workers are workers that multiple scripts can access, given that they follow the same origin policy (more on this in a later section named *Same origin policy*).

The API is a little different from dedicated workers, because these workers can be accessed by any script, so there's a need to manage all the connections via different ports baked into the `SharedWorker` object.

Setting up a shared worker

A shared worker can be created by calling the `SharedWorker` constructor and providing the name of the file as the argument:

```
const awesomeworker = new SharedWorker('myworker.js');
```

Here, we used the `SharedWorker` constructor to create an instance of a `sharedworker` object. Unlike with dedicated workers, you won't be able to see the HTTP network request in the browser made to the `myworker.js` file. This is important because the browser has to maintain only one instance of this file across multiple scripts calling this web worker:

```
// myworker.js
console.log('Hello world!');
```

Unlike dedicated workers, this does not log `Hello World!` in the main website's console. This is because shared workers do not get loaded into only that page. A shared worker is loaded once for every file accessing it. Therefore, it has its own console.

In Google Chrome, to debug a shared worker, open `chrome://inspect/#workers` after opening the page which is responsible for launching the shared worker. There, you'll have the option to debug it: ("Inspect" link)

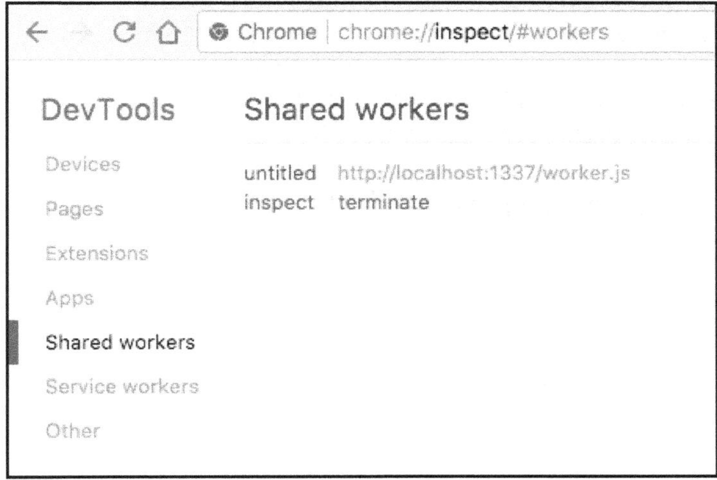

With that done, let's proceed to the guide to setting up listeners on shared workers.

Working with shared workers

Shared workers can communicate with their spawning script, listening to certain events which trigger when either of the scripts sends/receives a message. However, unlike dedicated workers, here we have to explicitly register the `onmessage` event on every connection.

Listening for messages on the main script

Here, unlike with dedicated workers, we have to add the `onmessage` event on the port property which is available on the shared worker object:

```
// script.js

const awesomeworker = new SharedWorker('myworker.js');
awesomeworker.port.start(); // important
awesomeworker.port.addEventListener('message', e => { // notice the .port
    console.log('Shared worker says .. ', e.data);
});
```

This event is triggered whenever our `SharedWorker` replies to this particular script.

Notice the line `awesomeworker.port.start();`, which instructs the shared worker to interact with this script. When using `addEventListener`, it is mandatory to start the communication with the `port.start()` line from both files (worker and script) for two-way communication.

Listening for messages on the worker script

Similarly, `self` is defined here; however, `window` is not. So, you can use `self.addEventListener` or `addEventListener` (or just `onconnect = function()`):

```
// myworker.js
addEventListener('connect', e => {
    console.log(e.ports);
    const port = e.ports[0];
    port.start();
    port.addEventListener('message', event => {
        console.log('Some calling script says.. ', event.data);
    });
});
```

Here, the event contains the details about the ports our script is connected to. We pick up the connecting port and establish a connection with it.

Similar to our main script, we have to specify `port.start()` here for a successful communication between the two files.

Sending messages from parent scripts

Note that any script in the same origin (basically, same origin means that you're accessing it from multiple URLs covered under the same domain; for example, `https://www.google.co.in/` accessing `google.com/script.js` follows the same origin, but `facebook.com` accessing `google.com/script.js` does not. There will be more on same origin in a later section named *Same origin policy*) can access the shared worker in the same way our previous `script.js` accesses it, with the worker being in the same state for every file which accesses it.

Here's how you'll send a message from a script to a worker:

```
// script.js

const awesomeworker = new SharedWorker('myworker.js');
awesomeworker.port.start();
awesomeworker.port.postMessage("Hello from the other side!");
```

This is similar to dedicated workers, with the exception that we have to explicitly mention the port object here.

The `myworker.js` file looks like:

```
// myworker.js
addEventListener('connect', e => {
    console.log(e.ports);
    const port = e.ports[0];
    port.start();
    port.addEventListener('message', event => {
        console.log('Some calling script says.. ', event.data); // logs
        "Hello from the other side!"
    });
});
```

As mentioned previously, we need to do a `port.start()` to establish the communication between the worker and the main script if we use `addEventListener` to add the callbacks. Then we assign an event listener for `onmessage` for this particular port.

Finally, we just log to console what the calling script has to say to the worker.

Sending messages from the worker script

If you've recognized the difference between how we call methods in dedicated workers versus how we call them in shared workers, well done! Instead of just calling methods on `self`, we're calling all the dedicated web worker methods on the port object, which is how the worker distinguishes between so many scripts that (can possibly) talk to it:

```
// myworker.js
addEventListener('connect', e => {
    console.log(e.ports);
    const port = e.ports[0];
    port.start();
    port.addEventListener('message', event => {
        console.log('Some calling script says.. ', event.data);
        // some work
        port.postMessage("Hello ;)");
    });
});
```

It is exactly like the code above, but with the exception that this time our shared worker replies to whoever sent the message and says `Hello` to it.

If you have two instances of the HTML page which loads `script.js` (that is, the new `SharedWorker`) running, both have separate port connections with the shared worker.

Error handling

Here, error handling is a bit tricky. Since the error can occur anywhere in the script by any port (any parent file), you have to manually send the error to every port. But for that, you'll have to store the ports, as well (when they're connected). Here's how it should look:

```
// myworker.js

const ports = [];

addEventListener('connect', e => {
    const port = e.ports[0];
    ports.push(port); // assemble all connections
    port.start();
```

```
    // .. other info
});

addEventListener('error', e => {
    console.log(e); // Info about error
    ports.forEach(port => port.postMessage({type: 'error', res: e}));
});
```

Here you can see that we are manually sending the error information to every parent file. Thereafter, you can handle the error in the parent file itself.

As a side note, it is good practice to have access to all connections in an array inside your shared worker. It might be helpful in some cases, such as when you want different pages to communicate with each other!

Terminating a shared worker connection

You can terminate a parent's connection from the shared worker, or completely shut down the shared worker. However, the latter can only be done by the worker's JS. The following sections talk about how you can terminate a single parent's connection with the worker.

Terminating a single parent-worker connection

When this code is called, the connection between the parent and worker is shut down, and you'll no longer be able to make use of that worker object to post messages:

```
// script.js

const awesomeworker = new SharedWorker('myworker.js');
awesomeworker.port.start();

// some processing and some work

awesomeworker.port.close();
awesomeworker.port.postMessage("Are you still alive?"); // does not work |
no effect
```

Although the worker still lives, it loses its connection from the script which calls `.port.close()`.

After the connection is closed, the worker won't be able to send/receive messages from the main script. However, the main script can always call the shared web worker again by creating a new instance with the `new SharedWorker` constructor.

Terminating a shared worker completely

A shared worker can itself be permanently terminated by calling `self.close()` inside its JS. You can also send a message from the parent script to kill the worker:

```
// script.js

const awesomeworker = new SharedWorker('myworker.js');
awesomeworker.port.start();

awesomeworker.port.postMessage({type: 'cmd', action: 'die'});
```

We simply sent a message from our main script to our shared worker and passed the message that the shared worker should be terminated permanently.

The worker file looks like:

```
// myworker.js

addEventListener('connect', e => {
    const port = e.ports[0];
    port.start();
    port.addEventListener('message', event => {
        if(event.data.type == 'cmd' && event.data.action == 'die') {
            self.close(); // terminates worker
        }
    });
});
```

After verifying that the main script really wants to terminate the worker for all instances, the worker calls the `close` method on itself, which terminates it.

Introduction to inline web workers

It is possible to create a web worker from a single file without actually having a separate JS file for your web worker. However, I still recommend that you create a different file for your web workers, for the sake of clarity of code and to make it more modular. Modularity is always preferred in programming.

We can make use of `blob` URLs to actually point data in memory to a URL, and then load the `blob` URL instead of an actual file URL. Since this URL is generated dynamically only on the user's computer, you do not need to create a separate file for that particular web worker. Here's how we'll do that:

```
const blob = new Blob(['(',
function() {
    // web worker code here
}.toString(),
')()'], { type: 'application/javascript' }));

const url = URL.createObjectURL(blob); // gives a url of kind
blob:http://....
const awesomeworker = new Worker(url);
```

It sometimes makes it easy to quickly fire a small web worker. However, this approach won't work for shared web workers. You'll need to have a separate file for them. This is because `SharedWorker` relies on the fact that all instances are loaded from one single file. However, creating a URL for blob data creates different URLs every time. So two pages, even if they have the same JS code, would have different URLs, and hence, different instances of `SharedWorker`.

Same origin policy

Earlier, I said a couple of times that shared workers will be available only to those parent files which share the same origin. What does that mean?

Let us consider the URL `http://www.packtpub.com/all`.

Here's a table demonstrating which URLs will be of the same origin with this domain, and which won't be:

New URL	**Same Origin**	**Reason**
`http://www.packtpub.com/support`	Yes	-
`http://www.packtpub.com/account/abc/xyz`	Yes	-
`https://www.packtpub.com/all`	No	Different protocol
`http://username:password@www.packtpub.com/all`	Yes	-
`http://www.packtpub.com:8000/somepage`	No	Different port number
`http://packtpub.com/somepage`	No	Different host

`http://dev.packtpub.com/somepage`	No	Different host

By now, I believe that you will be able to guess what makes something the same origin and what does not. Yes, you're right! The same host, port, and protocol make two URLs under the same origin. For listed URLs which have their answers as yes, only those URLs will be able to access the shared worker spun by `http://www.packtpub.com/all`.

Working with service workers

Service workers! They finally give developers precise control of the network layer by creating a network proxy in JavaScript. Using service workers, you can intercept and modify network resource requests, handle how caching is done, and respond appropriately when the user's network is down.

Let us show, step-by-step, how to set up a service worker and its associated methods.

Prerequisites for service workers

Prerequisites for service workers are:

- Because service workers are so powerful (almost like a network proxy) to avoid certain attacks, they're only available for domains running on HTTPS. However, they run fine on `localhost`, as well.
- They heavily depend on promises, which we've already covered in depth in *Chapter 4, Asynchronous Programming*.

Checking for browser support

It is easy to check whether a client's browser supports service workers or not:

```
if('serviceWorker' in navigator) {
    // service worker available
    // lets code
}
```

Here, I'll assume that a service worker is available in the user's browser, to avoid unnecessary code indentations every time.

The service worker life cycle

The following figure illustrates how a service worker lives:

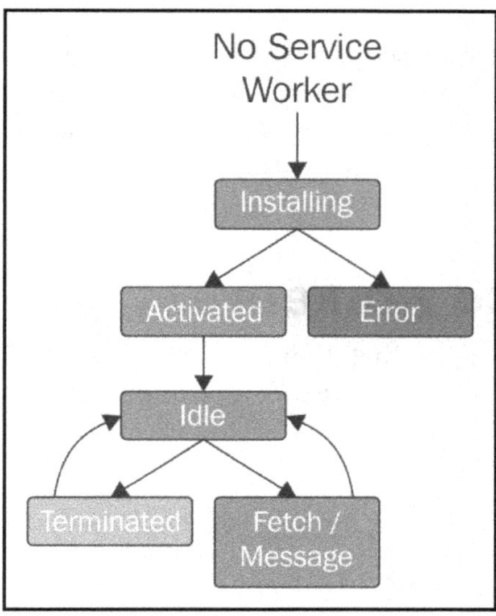

It is clear from the diagram that first a service worker needs to be installed. Then it triggers certain events which we can catch in our code to handle different stuff. Let us now discuss how to implement all of these steps, in detail.

Registering a service worker

First, your main script has to register the service worker to the browser. Here's how:

```
navigator.serviceWorker.register('/sw.js')
.then(reg => console.log(reg))
.catch(err => console.log(err));
```

The `reg` object is associated with information about the registration of your service worker.

A service worker registration code can be safely run multiple times. If already registered, the browser will not re-register it.

You can debug service workers here: **Chrome-->Inspect-->Service Workers.**

Note that a service worker script's scope is the scope where it is located. For example, the preceding file is located in the root directory (`localhost/sw.js`), so it can intercept all `localhost/*` requests. If it were located in, say, `localhost/directory/sw.js`, then it would be able to intercept only `localhost/directory/*` requests.

Installing service workers

Once your worker is registered, an install event is triggered inside your service worker file. Here, we'll set up caching of our resources. A lot of new terms are coming your way; hold tight:

```
// sw.js

self.addEventListener('install', e => {
    e.waitUntil(async function() {
        const cache = await caches.open('cacheArea');
        await cache.addAll(['/', '/styles/main.css', '/styles/about.css']);
    }());
});
```

Okay! What happened?

1. We added an install event listener to our `sw.js` file, which is triggered when our service worker is registered.
2. `e.waitUntil` accepts a promise (and we do give it a promise; remember that the `async function` returns a promise, and we invoked that function, as well).
3. Then we have something known as **CacheStorage** in browsers. We add resources to the cache by naming that cache and then using the `addAll` method to add the resources we want to cache.
4. We pass an array of all the files/paths we want to add to our cache storage.
5. The installation event is over.

It is completely optional to set up caching inside the installation event itself. We can do it later, after the install event, as well. For example, you can set up caching on the go when fetching new resources.

Fetching with service workers

Once everything is ready, you should be able to intercept requests with your service workers with the `fetch` event, in the following way:

```
self.addEventListener('fetch', e => {
    e.respondWith(async function() {
        const response = await caches.match(e.request);
        if(response) {
            return response;
        }
        return fetch(e.request);
  }());
});
```

Hang on! Let's see what happened here:

1. This listener will be fired whenever the browser makes a fetch request under its registration scope (we discussed that earlier).
2. `respondWith` also accepts a promise, which we gave it.
3. Then, we check whether or not the requested file is already present in our cache (using `catches.match(e.request)`). If it is, we return the cached file directly. If not, we use the fetch API (we discussed this in the previous chapter) to fetch the response, and the execution continues.

You can also console-log `e.request` and play around with it a little to modify the request. It gives the developer of the site immense power over his own site, and thus should not be handled by anyone else. This is the reason service workers are available only over the HTTPS protocol, to avoid a man-in-the-middle attack.

Service workers are a relatively new technology, and a lot of work is going on in their spec. Check out ;`http://bit.ly/serviceworkers` for any updates.

Summary

So, finally, we've had the chance to take a look at web workers and service workers and the great parts of the multi-threading environment provided by JavaScript! While service workers are the future of progressive web apps, web workers will be there to back them for any high-load task.

Combine these techs in just the right way, and everything seems possible! In the next chapter, we're going to take a look at very interesting concepts introduced in JavaScript for the first time: shared memory and atomics.

12
Shared Memory and Atomics

Let's go to low-level memory stuff! This chapter is going to be a bit advanced, but interesting. I'll try to make it as simple and understandable as possible.

With that out of the way, let's get to what we've FINALLY in JavaScript! Low-level memory access, multi-threading, atomics, shared memory, and all that cool and powerful stuff. But, as someone said, with great power comes great responsibility. Let's go!

We'll cover the following things in this chapter:

- Basics of memory management in computers
- What is shared memory?
- Using `SharedArrayBuffer`
- Introduction to parallel programming
- Problems when multiple threads access one memory location
- What are atomics?
- Performing atomic operations
- Atomic APIs in JavaScript
- Using parallel programming the right way

Basics of memory

We have to understand a little about how memory works in order to appreciate the significance of `SharedArrayBuffer` in JavaScript.

Think of memory as a collection of a lot of drawers in a big almirah kind of structure, where you can open a drawer and put something in it. Every drawer has its own maximum capacity.

Every drawer also has a sticker associated with it, which has a unique number on it that helps you to note down which drawer has data and which doesn't. When the time comes to access that data, you are supplied with the numbered drawer and you can take out data accordingly.

Now, let us start by understanding the basics of memory storage. Suppose I want to store a number, say, 100, in memory. First of all, we need to convert this number into binary, because that is what computers understand, and it is easy for them to store:

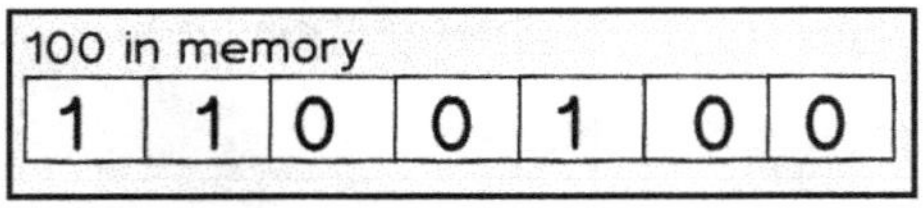

100 in memory

1	1	0	0	1	0	0

The preceding figure is a binary representation of the number 100 and is how it is stored in memory.

Easy! In a similar manner, we can store more complicated data, such as letters, by converting them to numbers (called ASCII values), and then storing those numbers directly, instead of letters. Similarly, an image (assumed to be black and white) can be stored by, say, storing the brightness levels of each pixel floating point number.

Abstraction of memory management

Memory management means that you're actually interacting directly with the hardware to store/update/free blocks of memory yourself from your code. Most higher level programming languages take away the memory management from the developers.

This is because managing memory is hard. It really is! In complicated programs, humans are bound to make mistakes and cause a ton of problems, not limited to memory leaks (which is the easiest mistake someone can make).

Of course, this abstraction comes at a performance cost. But compared with the security, readability, and convenience advantages, this is a fair deal.

JavaScript also manages memory automatically. The JavaScript engine is responsible for registering memory whenever a new variable is created, freeing the memory when it is no longer needed, and so on. Imagine managing memory for a **closure** program yourself! Even if the program is a bit complicated, it is very easy to lose track of which variables to keep in memory and which ones to discard, even after function execution ends. JavaScript to the rescue!

Garbage collection

JavaScript is a garbage collected language. What that means is that a JavaScript engine will occasionally fire something called a garbage collector, which looks for unused and inaccessible references in memory for the program and clears them, making the memory available for storing other data.

Garbage collectors make life a lot easier, but add a bit of overhead in performance-critical applications. Say you are coding a 3D game where you want very high **Frames Per Second** (**FPS**) on not so good hardware.

You might see that the results are extremely good for a game coded in C/C++, as compared to a garbage collected language like Java. This is because when you're playing the game, garbage collectors might fire off even when it is unnecessary, which wastes some resources that could've been used by the rendering thread.

Manually managing memory

Languages such as C/C++ are on their own in terms of memory management. In such languages, you have to allocate the memory and de-allocate it all by yourself. This is the reason why C/C++ are so fast--because they're very close to the hardware, and almost no abstraction is there. But that makes it painful to write complex applications because things can slip out of hand real quick.

There is something called as **WebAssembly**, which is the compiled form of a JavaScript alternative on the web. C/C++ code can be compiled down to WebAssembly, which is in some cases 100-200% faster than native JavaScript!

WebAssembly is going to be the future of the web because of its speed and multiple types of language support. However, it'll again require you to manage memory yourself, as, at the end of the day, C/C++ is what you'll need to write your code in.

Manually managing memory is hard. It is hard to know when to clear off the part of memory you don't require in bigger programs. Do it early, and you break the application. Do it late, and you are out of memory. This is the reason abstraction is good in a lot of cases.

What is shared memory?

Let's suppose we are working on a real-time performance-critical application, which is the reason we're so concerned about this interesting topic. Suppose I have two web workers running in the background, and I want to share some data from one worker to another. Web workers run independently on separate OS-level threads and have no idea about each other.

One way is to make use of `postMessage` to transfer messages between web workers, as we saw in the last chapter. However, this is slow.

Another way is to transfer the object to another worker completely; however, if you remember, that makes the object which is transferred inaccessible from the worker which sent it.

The solution to this problem is `SharedArrayBuffer`.

Introduction to SharedArrayBuffer

The `SharedArrayBuffer` is the way to create a memory store which is accessible to all workers simultaneously. Now, if you've been reading keenly, you will have understood something mischievous that can happen once something like a shared memory store is allowed to exist.

If you remember, the only reason workers didn't have direct access to `DOM` was because the DOM API is not thread-safe, and could cause problems like deadlocks and race conditions. And if you were able to judge that the same thing might happen here, you're right! But that's a topic for a later section (*The race condition*).

Let's get back to `SharedArrayBuffer`. So what's different from `ArrayBuffer`?

Well, `SharedArrayBuffer` is pretty much the `ArrayBuffer` which is available to a lot of scripts. You just have to create `SharedArrayBuffer` in one place and use `postMessage` to post it to other workers (and not transfer it!).

You should not transfer it because you'll then lose ownership of the `SharedArrayBuffer`. When you post it, only the reference of the buffer is automatically passed and becomes available to all the other scripts:

```
const sab = new SharedArrayBuffer(1024);
worker.postMessage(sab); // DO NOT TRANSFER: worker.postMessage(sab,
[sab]);
```

Once you do that, all the workers will be able to access, read, and write to `SharedArrayBuffer`. Take a look at the representation as follows:

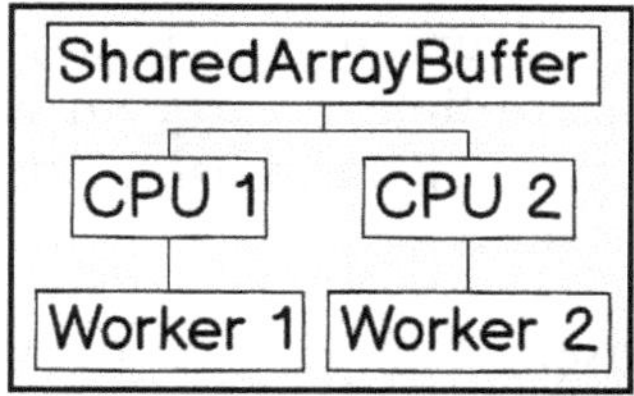

This is a rough representation of how you might imagine `SharedArrayBuffer` is connected to the memory under the hood. Let's assume each thread is spawned on a different CPU, for now.

Understanding parallel programming

Parallel programming, as the name suggests, is just a program running in such a way that instances of that program are running simultaneously multiple times.

Concurrent programming, on the other hand, is very similar to parallel programming, but with the difference that tasks never happen together.

Parallel versus concurrent programming

To understand the difference between parallel and concurrent programming, let us consider an example.

Suppose there's a competition to eat candies put on two plates. Plates are at a distance of five meters from each other. Let's say you're the only player for now, and the constraint is that you have to keep the number of differences in candies on both plates to less than two.

What will you do here? You have to eat from plate one, run five meters to plate two, eat from plate two, run five meters again to plate one, and so on.

Now, let's assume you have got a friend. Now, both of you can choose a plate and start eating your own candies.

Try to relate it to concurrent programming and parallel programming, respectively. In the first example, you are the CPU's core, which is running here and there, again and again, between two threads (plates). You are running fast, but, no matter how hard you try, you cannot eat from both plates at the same time due to your physical limits. Similarly, the CPU in concurrent programming is doing both of the tasks, but instead of doing them simultaneously, it is doing both in chunks.

In the next example, for parallel programming, your friend acts like another CPU, which is handling the other thread completely. This way, each of you only have to execute your own thread. This is parallelism.

If that makes sense, then let us get into parallel programming, the thing which web workers give us, and how to make use of shared memory with parallel programming to actually make things faster and not slow them down (because that happens a lot of times, when you do it incorrectly).

Myth-busting--Parallel computation is always faster

It seems so intuitive to say that parallel computation should always be faster than computing on a single thread. Like spawning two threads should, intuitively, almost halve the computation time. Not only is this numerically wrong, but parallel computing creates garbage results if not done properly.

To understand this, consider a man who is given a task to transfer a pile of blocks from one place to another:

He does this work at some speed. Putting another man with him might sound like doubling the speed of the work, but the two might actually crash into each other on their way and make things slower instead of faster.

This actually happens a lot of times when parallelism is implemented incorrectly, as we shall see now.

Let's count one billion!

To verify that parallel computing, if set up wrongly, is actually garbage, let us count to one billion using a single-threaded and multi-threaded environment in JavaScript.

Let us first try single-threaded counting:

```
// Main thread

const sharedMem = new SharedArrayBuffer(4);

function countSingleThread(limit) {
    const arr = new Uint32Array(sharedMem);
    for(let i=0; i<limit; i++) {
        arr[0] = arr[0] + 1;
    }
}

const now = performance.now();
countSingleThread(1000000000);
console.log(`Time Taken: ${performance.now() - now}`);
```

On my MacBook Air, it takes ~*2606* milliseconds for this program to run. That is roughly *2.6* seconds:

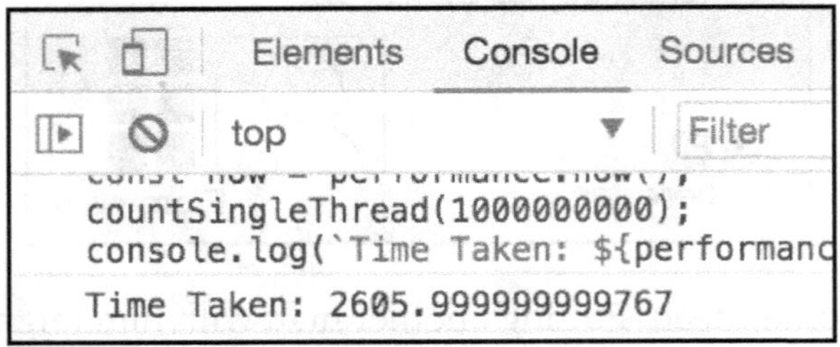

Let us try to split the code among two workers now, and see what happens:

```
// Main thread

const sharedMem = new SharedArrayBuffer(4);
const workers = [new Worker('worker.js'), new Worker('worker.js')];
let oneWorkerDone = false;
const now = performance.now();

for(let i=0;i<2;i++) {
  workers[i].postMessage({message: 'sab', memory: sharedMem});

  workers[i].addEventListener('message', data => {
      if(!oneWorkerDone) {
        oneWorkerDone = true;
      } else {
        console.log("Both workers done. The memory is: ", new
        Uint32Array(sharedMem))
        console.log(`Time taken: ${performance.now()-now}`)
      }
  });

  workers[i].postMessage({cmd: 'start', iterations: 500000000});
}
```

Alright! So what the heck is going on here? The following is an explanation:

1. We created a `SharedArrayBuffer` in order to create a memory storage area which can be accessed simultaneously by both of the spawned web workers.
2. The size of `SharedArrayBuffer` is `4` because, to add numbers to the integer array, we'll cast it to `Uint32Array`, which has a size in multiples of `4`.
3. We started two web workers from the same file.

4. We gave them access to `SharedArrayBuffer`.
5. We're listening in the main script when both workers say they're done.
6. We are sending 500 million iterations to each worker, thus splitting the work among these two threads.

Let us now look at what `worker.js` looks like:

```
// worker.js
let sharedMem;

addEventListener('message', ({data}) => {
  //console.log(data);
    if(data.message == 'sab') {
        sharedMem = data.memory;
        console.log('Memory ready');
    }
    if(data.cmd == 'start') {
      console.log('Iterations ready');
        startCounting(data.iterations);
    }
});

function startCounting(limit) {
    const arr = new Uint32Array(sharedMem);
    for(let i=0;i<limit;i++) {
        arr[0] += 1;
    }
    postMessage('done')
}
```

In `worker.js`, we do the following:

1. Listen for messages from the main script.
2. Check if the message says to store `SharedArrayBuffer`; if it does, we store it.
3. If the message says to start the iterations, we start by first converting it to `Uint32Array`.
4. After iterations, we send a nice 'done' message to the main script to inform it that we're done.

Expectation: The program will have a speed-up of around 2x because each thread has to do half of the work. Also, we expect the final value to be one billion.

Reality: Test #1 is as follows.

Running the preceding code for the first time produces the following result:

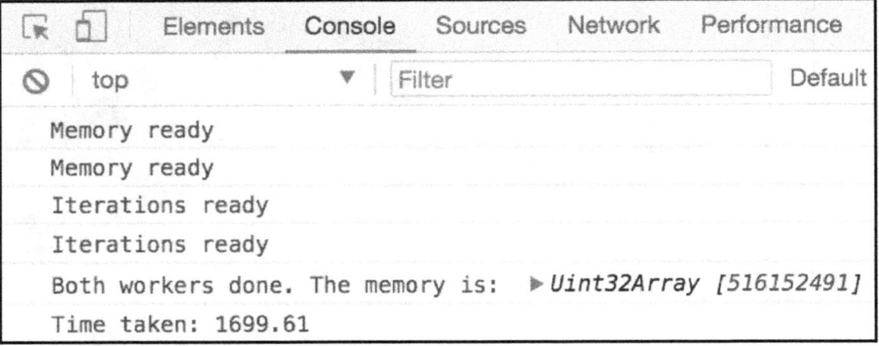

Test #2 is as follows.

Running the preceding code for the second time produces the following result:

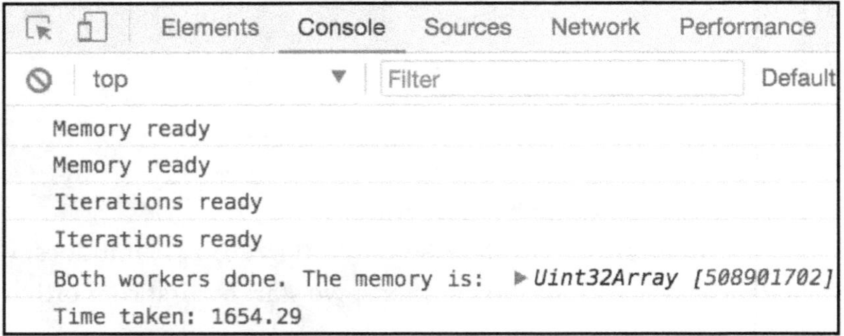

Test #3 is as follows.

Running the preceding code for the third time produces the following result:

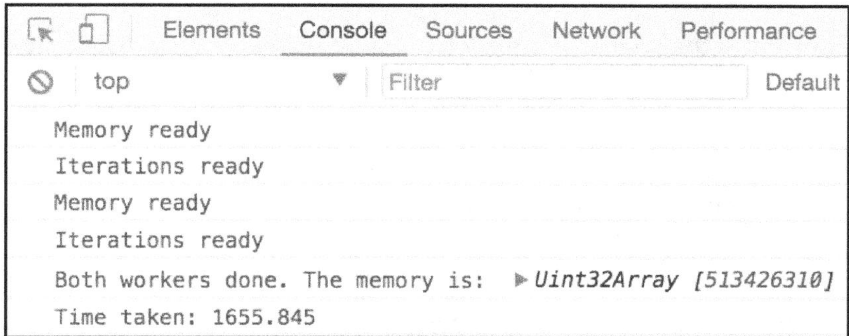

I've got garbage values! Every time I run the program, I get different values, near 500 million. Why is this so?

The race condition

The garbage values which were there in the immediately previous two screenshots represent a classic race condition example. Do you remember the first image I showed you in the *Introduction to SharedArrayBuffer* section? Remember the `SharedArrayBuffer` linking to **CPU 1** and **CPU 2,** which links to **Worker 1** and **Worker 2**? Well, it turns out it's not completely correct.

Here's how the actual setup is in your machine:

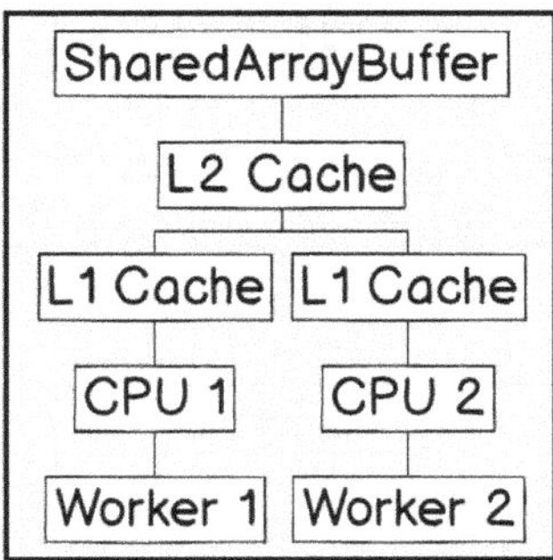

The problem arises here. Race condition means that **CPU 1** fetches the shared memory and sends it to **Worker 1**. Meanwhile, **CPU 2** also fetches it, but doesn't know that **CPU 1** is already working on it. So, by the time **Worker 1** has changed the value from *0* to *1*, **CPU 2**, that is, **Worker 2**, is still fetching the value 0.

Worker 1 then updates the shared memory to a value of 1, and then **Worker 2** updates its own copy to a value of 1 (because it doesn't know that **CPU 1** has already updated it to 1), and then writes it again to the shared memory.

Here, we've successfully wasted two computations, which required only one. That was a quick example of how not to do parallelism:

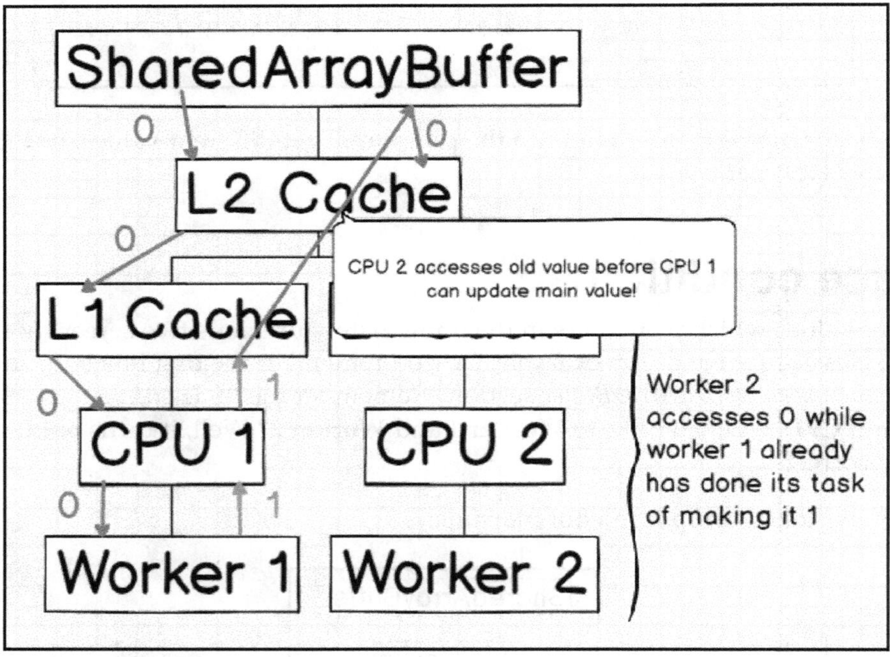

How do we fix this? Atomics (we will come back to this problem later in the chapter, in the section *Fixing one billion count with atomics*).

What are atomics?

What are atomics? Atomics, or, more precisely, an atomic operation, is an operation which happens in one go, not in steps. It is like an atom --indivisible (although an atom is technically divisible, let's not destroy the analogy).

An atomic operation is a single operation as seen by all other working threads. It just happens immediately. It is like the execution of one machine code, which is either not done yet or is completed. There is no in-between.

In a nutshell, something being atomic means that only one operation can be done on it at a time. For example, updating a variable can be made atomic. This can be used to avoid a race condition.

Information about lock and mutex

When I said updating a variable can be made atomic, it means that during the time a thread is accessing that memory, no other thread should be allowed to access it. This is only possible when you introduce a lock or a mutex (mutual exclusion) on the variable being accessed. This way, the other thread knows that the variable is in use and it should wait for the lock to be released.

This is how you make an operation atomic. But this sense of security also comes at a cost. Atomic locking is not an operation which will take negligible time, so it definitely involves some overhead.

Do it a billion times, and you're probably screwed (we'll see that soon in *Fixing one billion count with atomics*).

Atomics in JavaScript

JavaScript has an `Atomics` object, which provides us with exactly the functionality we discussed previously. However, it is quite limited, in the sense that you can only do addition, subtraction, bitwise AND, bitwise OR, bitwise XOR, and storing.

Other features can be built on top of these, and, in future, there will be libraries providing that. For now, let's learn about the natively available methods.

Using the Atomics.load(typedArray, index) method

The `Atomics.load` method returns the value inside a typed array at a particular index value. Here's how to use it:

```
const sab = new SharedArrayBuffer(1);
const arr = new Uint8Array(sab);
arr[0] = 5;

console.log(Atomics.load(arr, 0));
```

The preceding code is just a thread-safe way to access `arr[0]`.

This outputs:

```
5
```

Using the Atomics.add(typedArray, index, value) method

`Atomics.add` is a way to add a particular value to a particular index in a typed array. It is fairly simple to understand and write:

```
const sab = new SharedArrayBuffer(1);
const arr = new Uint8Array(sab);
arr[0] = 5;

console.log(Atomics.add(arr, 0, 10));
console.log(Atomics.load(arr, 0));
```

`Atomics.add` is, again, a thread-safe way of performing `arr[0] += 10`.

This outputs:

```
5
15
```

`Atomics.add` returns the old value at that index. The value is updated at that index after the command is run.

Using the Atomics.sub(typedArray, index, value) method

`Atomics.sub` is a way to subtract a particular value from a particular index in a typed array. It is also fairly simple to use:

```
const sab = new SharedArrayBuffer(1);
const arr = new Uint8Array(sab);
arr[0] = 5;

console.log(Atomics.sub(arr, 0, 2));
console.log(Atomics.load(arr, 0));
```

`Atomics.sub` is, again, a thread-safe way of doing `arr[0] -= 2`.

This outputs:

```
5
3
```

`Atomics.sub` returns the old value at that index. The value is updated at that index after the command is run.

Using the Atomics.and(typedArray, index, value) method

`Atomics.and` performs a bitwise AND between the value at that particular index in the typed array and the value you supplied:

```
const sab = new SharedArrayBuffer(1);
const arr = new Uint8Array(sab);
arr[0] = 5; // 5 is 0101 in binary.

Atomics.and(arr, 0, 12); // 12 is 1100 in binary
console.log(Atomics.load(arr, 0));
```

`Atomics.and` here performs a bitwise AND between `arr[0]` and the number `12`.

This outputs:

```
4
```

How bitwise AND works

Suppose we want to take a bitwise AND of 5 and 12:

1. Covert both numbers to binary; 5 is 0101 and 12 is 1100.
2. Bitwise AND performs the `AND` operation bit by bit, starting from the first bit:
   5 & 12
   0 && 1 = 0
   1 && 1 = 1
   0 && 0 = 0
   1 && 0 = 0
3. Thus, *5 && 12 = 0100,* which is 4.

Using the Atomics.or(typedArray, index, value) method

Similar to bitwise AND, `Atomics.or` method performs a bitwise OR:

```
const sab = new SharedArrayBuffer(1);
const arr = new Uint8Array(sab);
arr[0] = 5; // 5 is 0101 in binary.

Atomics.or(arr, 0, 12); // 12 is 1100 in binary
console.log(Atomics.load(arr, 0));
```

Here, `Atomics.or` method performed a bitwise OR between `arr[0]` and the number `12`.

The output is:

```
13
```

How bitwise OR works

Suppose we want to take a bitwise OR of 5 and 12:

1. Covert both numbers to binary; 5 is 0101 and 12 is 1100
2. Bitwise OR performs an OR operation bit by bit, starting from the first bit:
   5 | 12
   0 || 1 = 1
   1 || 1 = 1
   0 || 0 = 0
   1 || 0 = 1
3. Thus, *5 | 12 = 1101* which is 13.

Using the Atomics.xor(typedArray, index, value) method

Again, `Atomics.xor` method performs a bitwise XOR operation, which is an exclusive OR (that is, it is an OR gate which gives `0` when both inputs are `1`)

```
const sab = new SharedArrayBuffer(1);
const arr = new Uint8Array(sab);
arr[0] = 5; // 5 is 0101 in binary.

Atomics.xor(arr, 0, 12); // 10 is 1100 in binary
console.log(Atomics.load(arr, 0));
```

`Atomics.xor` here performed a XOR operation between `arr[0]` and the number `10`.

This outputs:

```
9
```

How bitwise XOR works

Suppose we want to take a bitwise XOR of 5 and 12:

1. Covert both numbers to binary; 5 is 0101 and 12 is 1100.
2. Bitwise XOR performs an XOR operation bit by bit, starting from the first bit:
   5 ^ 12
   0 ^ 1 = 1
   1 ^ 1 = 0
   0 ^ 0 = 0
   1 ^ 0 = 1
3. Thus, *5 ^ 12 = 1001*, which is 9.

With all the knowledge we required about atomics, let's hop back to our one billion count problem and see a possible fix.

Fixing one billion count with atomics

Now we know the reason for our garbage value, and, with atomics, it should be easy to fix the problem. Right? Wrong.

There is a massive performance penalty on using atomic locking a billion times. Let's look at our updated `worker.js` code now:

```
// worker.js
let sharedMem;

addEventListener('message', ({data}) => {
  //console.log(data);
    if(data.message == 'sab') {
        sharedMem = data.memory;
        console.log('Memory ready');
    }
    if(data.cmd == 'start') {
      console.log('Iterations ready');
        startCounting(data.iterations);
    }
});

function startCounting(limit) {
    const arr = new Uint32Array(sharedMem);
    for(let i=0;i<limit;i++) {
        Atomics.add(arr, 0, 1);
    }
    postMessage('done')
}
```

This is similar to our previous implementation of the problem, with the change being that instead of adding it directly to the array, we are performing an atomic operation so that the value isn't changed by the other thread while one thread is adding value to it.

Sure, it is a beautiful fix. And it works, as well:

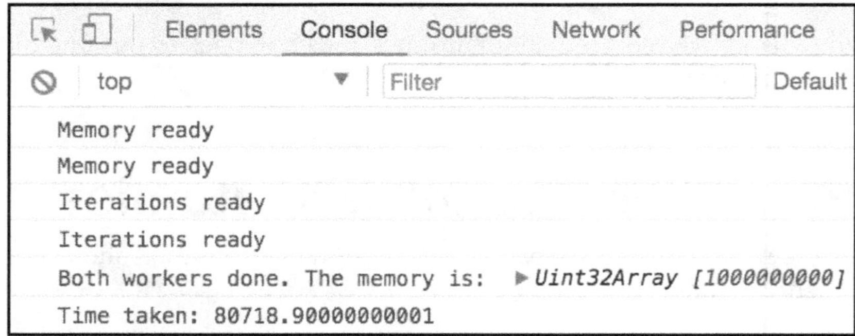

But look at that time: 80 seconds! That is the penalty you get when you lock and unlock over a memory one billion times.

Single threaded is faster, because it can access the local variable values from the register really quickly and use them. Our performance is slow because we're getting the reference to shared memory down, locking it, incrementing it, putting it up, and unlocking it.

Let's read that again. Single threaded is faster because it can access the local variable values from the register really quickly and use them. Can we do something about this? Let's see!

The optimized fix

Why not combine the good parts of atomics and the good parts of the speed of local variables sitting in the CPU register? Here we are:

```
// worker.js
let sharedMem;

addEventListener('message', ({data}) => {
  //console.log(data);
    if(data.message == 'sab') {
        sharedMem = data.memory;
        console.log('Memory ready');
    }
    if(data.cmd == 'start') {
      console.log('Iterations ready');
        startCounting(data.iterations);
    }
});

function startCounting(limit) {
    const arr = new Uint32Array(sharedMem);
    let count = 0;
    for(let i=0;i<limit;i++) {
        count += 1;
    }
    Atomics.add(arr, 0, count);
    postMessage('done')
}
```

Here, from our last implementation, we took `Atomics.add` out of the loop to avoid calling it a billion times. Instead, we performed the work assigned to this web worker inside a local variable, and updated the memory with atomics only when we were done. This ensures no overwrite by two threads, in case they finish at the same moment. It's time to see the output.

Look at these awesome results:

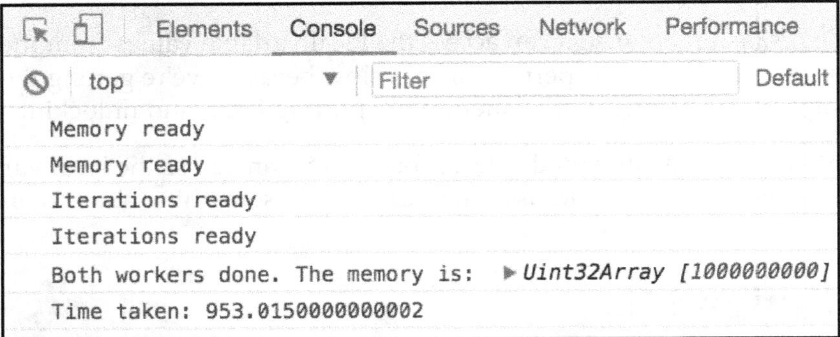

It is less than a second! That is about a 2.5 times gain by using just two workers! When we implemented parallel programming correctly, we were able to defeat our projected speed-up of 2x and shoot it to about 2.5x!

Hang on. The story doesn't end here. Let's add `4` workers and see what happens:

```
// Main Script

const sharedMem = new SharedArrayBuffer(4);
const workers = [new Worker('worker.js'), new Worker('worker.js'), new
Worker('worker.js'), new Worker('worker.js')];
let workersDone = 0;

const now = performance.now();

for(let i=0;i<2;i++) {
  workers[i].postMessage({message: 'sab', memory: sharedMem});

  workers[i].addEventListener('message', data => {
      if(++workersDone == 4) { // don't worry. this is thread-safe ;)
        console.log("All workers done. The memory is: ", new
Uint32Array(sharedMem))
        console.log(`Time taken: ${performance.now()-now}`)
      }
  });

  workers[i].postMessage({cmd: 'start', iterations:
1000000000/workers.length});
}
```

Excited to see the results? So am I! Let's see:

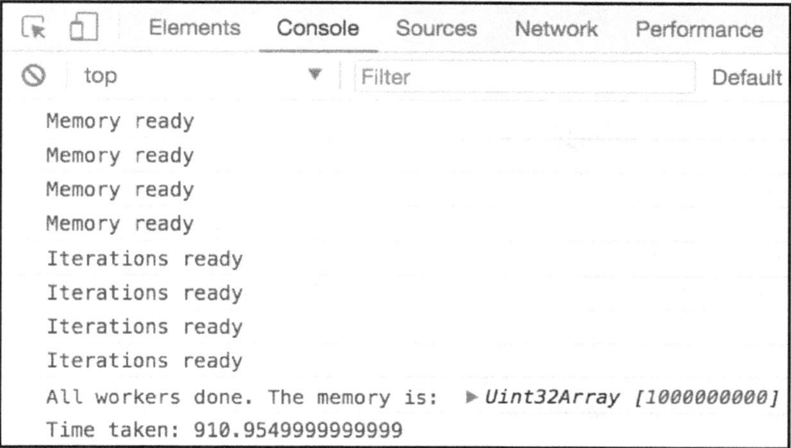

Uh oh. Hmm, that doesn't seem like a very impressive performance gain. Going from one thread to two threads was a huge boost. Why is going from two to four, not one?

Let's take a look at the **Network** tab:

worker.js	200	javascript	script.js:4	687 B	115 ms
worker.js	200	javascript	script.js:4	687 B	115 ms
worker.js	200	javascript	script.js:4	687 B	116 ms
worker.js	200	javascript	script.js:4	687 B	116 ms

Eureka moment! It looks like we're spending 462 ms out of 911 ms of total program execution on just downloading the `worker.js` file! This even excludes the time for compilation of every individual script to machine code, which the JavaScript engine performs once it downloads.

Unfortunately, that is the end of what we can do from our end. Now it's browser's task to optimize the thing that if a single file is called again and again in the web worker, it should pickup compiled file from cache so it can actually use an already compiled instance of one file instead of downloading it three more times and then compiling them again.

In future, if Chrome optimizes according to the preceding suggestion, we can say it takes around ~*120* ms instead of 462 ms of downloading and compiling.

Therefore, our script, in the near future, will take around ~570 ms to count to one billion. That is a performance gain of 500% over a single thread. That is multi-threading in JavaScript for you, folks.

A peek into Spectre

On January 3, 2018, there was a fundamental flaw discovered with the CPU architecture we've been using for the past 20 years. This has shaken modern security to its roots. While the workings of Spectre and Meltdown are highly complicated (and deeply interesting, if you like the security field), what you have to know right now is that because of Spectre, all major browser vendors have disabled `SharedArrayBuffer` in browsers by default.

You can enable `SharedArrayBuffer` by going to `chrome://flags` and searching for `SharedArrayBuffer` and enabling it.

The reason for disabling `SharedArrayBuffer` is to mitigate Spectre, which is a dangerous but beautifully crafted exploit which requires a very precise measurement of time to attack. `SharedArrayBuffer` provides a way for multiple threads to be accessible to every thread, and atomics add more precision over the data available. This can be used to create highly precise clocks using `SharedArrayBuffer`, which can be used to carry out a Spectre attack.

Spectre basically exploits the fact that modern CPUs precompute a lot of things and put them in the cache. So, if you get ACCESS DENIED for a part of memory your program is not supposed to access way quicker than it's supposed to be, chances are, that particular block of memory is in the cache. Using beautifully crafted scripts, it is even possible to know which value is in the cache because your program is the one which put it there!

Ahh! It'll take a long chapter to actually have a little fun with Spectre and Meltdown. But that is for some other day, some other book. The takeaway from here is that at the time of writing this chapter, `SharedArrayBuffer` is not enabled in browsers by default. It will be enabled in the future, when proper patches are put in place by all browser vendors.

Here are some articles for people who find such stuff cool:

- How Spectre works: `http://www.i-programmer.info/news/149-security/11449-how-spectre-works.html`
- Spectre and Meltdown explained: `https://www.csoonline.com/article/3247868/vulnerabilities/spectre-and-meltdown-explained-what-they-are-how-they-work-whats-at-risk.html`

Till then, stay safe!

Summary

It wouldn't be wrong to say that this is now my favorite chapter, with *Chapter 4, Asynchronous Programming,* sliding down to number two. This technology is raw, fresh, and waiting to be explored.

We learned a lot of new stuff about ES2017 in this chapter, which, in the near future, will be the base of multi-threaded programs written in JavaScript. Well, that is it! You're now a good developer who knows a lot about ES2017 (that is, ES8) and a lot more about future tech, as well. Use your powers to make this world a good place!

Other Books You May Enjoy

If you enjoyed this book, you may be interested in these other books by Packt:

Learning JavaScript Data Structures and Algorithms - Second Edition
Loiane Groner

ISBN: 978-1-78528-549-3

- Declare, initialize, add, and remove items from arrays, stacks, and queues
- Get the knack of using algorithms such as DFS (Depth-first Search) and BFS (Breadth-First Search) for the most complex data structures
- Harness the power of creating linked lists, doubly linked lists, and circular linked lists
- Store unique elements with hash tables, dictionaries, and sets
- Use binary trees and binary search trees
- Sort data structures using a range of algorithms such as bubble sort, insertion sort, and quick sort

Object-Oriented JavaScript - Third Edition
Ved Antani, Stoyan Stefanov

ISBN: 978-1-78588-056-8

- Apply the basics of object-oriented programming in the JavaScript environment
- Use a JavaScript Console with complete mastery
- Make your programs cleaner, faster, and compatible with other programs and libraries
- Get familiar with Iterators and Generators, the new features added in ES6
- Find out about ECMAScript 6's Arrow functions, and make them your own
- Understand objects in Google Chrome developer tools and how to use them
- Use a mix of prototypal inheritance and copying properties in your workflow
- Apply reactive programming techniques while coding in JavaScript

Leave a review - let other readers know what you think

Please share your thoughts on this book with others by leaving a review on the site that you bought it from. If you purchased the book from Amazon, please leave us an honest review on this book's Amazon page. This is vital so that other potential readers can see and use your unbiased opinion to make purchasing decisions, we can understand what our customers think about our products, and our authors can see your feedback on the title that they have worked with Packt to create. It will only take a few minutes of your time, but is valuable to other potential customers, our authors, and Packt. Thank you!

Index

C

D

E

F

G

H

I

J

L

M

N

O

P

Q

R

www.ingramcontent.com/pod-product-compliance
Lightning Source LLC
Chambersburg PA
CBHW080628060326
40690CB00021B/4857

* 9 7 8 1 7 8 8 6 2 0 0 6 2 *